Pennine rails and trails

Key to front cover pictures

1 — A two-car Pacer train at Gauxholme

2 — Churn Milk Joan, a boundary stone on Midgley Moor

3 — The Calderdale Way above Mytholmroyd

4 — The paved road over Blackstone Edge

All cover shots by John Morrison

*Edwardian special — a 3ft gauge Bagnall 0-6-0 saddle tank engine
with an unusual load at "Dawson City" — Slack Bottom,
Heptonstall, in 1902. Shibden Museum Collection.*

Pennine rails and trails

*Exploring Calderdale and Rochdale
by train and foot*

With a foreword by MIKE HARDING

by

John Morrison

and

Lydia Speakman

Series Editor Stan Abbott

Pennine Rails and Trails

Published by Leading Edge Press and Publishing, the Old Chapel, Burtersett, Hawes, North Yorkshire, DL8 3PB.
☎ (0969) 667566

British Library Cataloguing in Publication Data

Morrison, John, *1951-*
    Pennine rails and trails (exploring Calderdale and
    Rochdale by train and foot). — (RailTrail Series)
    1. England. Pennines — Visitors' guides
    I. Title II. Speakman, Lydia III. Series
    914.2804858

    ISBN 0-948135-21-2

RailTrail series editor, and designer: Stan Abbott

Sketch maps by Gaynor Cole

Type: Leading Edge Press & Publishing, Pagefast Ltd

Colour reprographics: Impression, Leeds

Printed and bound in Great Britain by Ebenezer Baylis and Son Ltd, Worcester

RailTrail logo by Barbara Drew

Contents

Preface

THIS book has been produced as part of the celebrations to mark the 150th anniversary of the first railway across the Pennines. Various structures and significant dates in the line's history enjoy their 150th anniversaries during late 1990 and 1991.

Although the original trans-Pennine railway connected Manchester and Leeds by way of Brighouse and Wakefield, the various trails featured in this book are begun and ended by catching a train on the route now taken, which runs via Halifax.

The publishers are grateful to the Metropolitan District Councils of Calderdale and Rochdale for the assistance in the realisation of this project. Particular thanks are also due to Jane Brantom, David Nortcliffe, Frances Cummin, Colin Speakman, Doris Dyson, Jeff Fisher, Alice Longstaff, Roger Birch, Trevor Sutcliffe.

Maps

The maps which accompany the walks in this book are sketched for guidance only and are not to scale. The publishers strongly recommend that walkers also carry the relevant Ordance Survey sheet. The appropriate 1:50,000 series sheets are: nos. 103, 104 and 109. The 1:25,000 scale map of the South Pennines is also recommended.

We advise walkers to wear strong footwear, and carry waterproof clothing and provisions. A compass is also recommended, particularly on the upland sections. Observe the Country Code!

Photographs

The pictures in this book were all taken by John Morrison, unless otherwise credited.

Foreword

BY MIKE HARDING

Vice President of the Ramblers' Association

THE Pennines were my first playground and on long summer holidays from school I would walk the hills around Rochdale and Oldham, camping out above Chew Valley on "Pots and Pans" and cycling to Hollingworth Lake for a swim.

It was in the hills that I first learned of the beauty of the world and it was there, too, that I did my first courting and kissed my first girl.

Since then, I've walked to the foot of Everest and trekked down to the floor of the Grand Canyon, but the Pennine Hills always draw me back and there can be nothing more wonderful than lying on your back in the heather above Blackstone Edge on a hot summer's day, watching clouds chasing across the sky and hearing the song of a lark, a tiny, bubbling speck above you.

If this book helps you to get out and explore and discover some of the beauties of a landscape where man laboured in the smoky valleys and walked the hills on a Sunday, then it will have done what every good book should do. Enjoy your walking.

Mike Harding, August 1990

Mike Harding snips a ribbon to inaugurate the Settle & Carlisle Way, featured in a companion volume to this book

The engine of a goods train derailed at Todmorden in 1942 (Roger Birch collection)

THE Calder Valley line — the first railway to cross the Pennines — was a monumental piece of Victorian engineering. Between Manchester and Leeds the line goes through no fewer than 11 tunnels, and crosses 22 viaducts and 134 other bridges. Tunnelling totalled 5,432 yards, the Summit Tunnel at Littleborough being the longest at 2,885 yards.

The idea for a railway between Manchester and Leeds was first mooted in 1825 — the same year as the Stockton and Darlington Railway opened, and the Liverpool and Manchester Railway Company was formed. The chosen route closely followed the Rochdale Canal, which was opened in 1804.

The canal company fiercely opposed the proposed railway. George Stephenson — by this time famous as the engineer of the Stockton and Darlington and Liverpool and Manchester railways — and James Walker were appointed to survey the route. Their report was published in November 1830, though the line as eventually built was very different to that proposed in this report. For example, Stephenson originally hoped to cross the Pennines without having to bore tunnels.

Stephenson appointed Thomas Longridge Gooch as his assistant. Gooch eventually took on the responsibility for much of the surveying and most of the construction of the line. He had worked with Stephenson in the North East, on the Liverpool and Manchester and Bolton and Leigh Railways. So Gooch was well acquainted with drawing and field work when he came to the Pennine uplands.

His experiences reveal something of the demands — and hardships — of the early railway engineers. By day he spent his time surveying; by night he plotted his results and drew plans. The last levels were taken from the summit of the Rochdale Canal, working by torchlight. To keep within the time limit, two carriages — each with four horses — were hired to rush the plans, sections and books of reference to the Clerks of the Peace in Wakefield and Preston.

The first Bill was introduced into Parliament in February 1831, only to be thrown out in July. Here matters lay until 1835, when the railway company was reconstituted, and Stephenson was again appointed chief engineer.

The original plans were revised, and a new Bill was presented to Parliament the following year. Again there was fierce opposition from the Rochdale Canal Company and landowners. Despite this, however, the Bill was passed and received the Royal Assent on July 4. Some alterations to the route were authorised the following May, thereby establishing the route which was subsequently built.

Construction

Although George Stephenson characteristically tried to keep the gradients as easy as possible (even at the expense of great mileage) the Manchester to Leeds line was not an easy one to build.

The route ran from Manchester (Oldham Road), via Rochdale, Littleborough, Todmorden, Sowerby Bridge, Mirfield and Wakefield, to Normanton, where it joined the North Midland Rail-

Top: An L & Y train pulling out of Mytholmroyd station (Alice Longstaff collection)
Bottom: The Summit Tunnel fire of 1984 (Roger Birch collection)

way, over whose metals trains could then reach Leeds. By this route the distance between Manchester and Leeds was 62 miles. The shortest distance by rail between the two cities today is 48 miles, along the more direct route via Huddersfield.

By adopting this circuitous route, Stephenson was able to cross the Pennine watershed at a height of only 573 feet above sea level, using the Walsden valley. The railway was not the first transport system to take advantage of this pass. Keeping to the higher ground, the Romans used part of it for a road over Blackstone Edge. In later years the packhorse route of Reddyshore Scout Gate used the pass. In 1804 the Rochdale Canal was completed. Lastly, in 1824, the turnpike road was constructed near the canal.

Work on the Manchester to Littleborough section of the railway began in August 1837. The terminus was at Manchester Oldham Road, where the station was built on a viaduct to reduce the gradient. The booking office was at ground level, inside a large, rather plain three-storey office building. Construction of the terminus began in 1839 and took nearly a year.

It was Stephenson's idea to use the arches beneath the station as warehouses. He designed a wagon hoist capable of handling 1,000 tons per day for transferring wagons from one level to the other. Two hoists were built and gave good service until they were demolished in 1946 and 1947. Oldham Road was to be used as a passenger station for only four years; it became a goods station only when Manchester Victoria station opened on January 1, 1844.

Once past Miles Platting the line was built with a uniformly ascending gradient of about 1 in 155. It is remarkable to consider the long sweeping curves and lengthy straights of the Manchester and Leeds line, in contrast to the meander-

Platelayers working on the Summit Tunnel, c 1905 (Roger Birch collection)

Carriages line up to collect passengers outside Sowerby Bridge station (Roy Dyson)

ings of the other railways across the Pennines.

In 1845, A F Tait and Edwin Butterworth collaborated to produce a book of illustrations and a description of the route. This work provides some interesting facts and figures about the line and the places it served. About Rochdale, Butterworth wrote: "A small but commodious neat edifice was built as the station to serve the town which then had a population of 24,483."

Beyond Rochdale the railway was built level past Smithy Bridge. In later years water troughs were provided here, from which locomotives could collect water without stopping. From Smithy Bridge to the tunnel the line climbed at the easy gradient of 1 in 330.

Littleborough, now a small and pleasant town, was then no more than a village. The first station here may have been alongside Windybank Lock on the Rochdale Canal, linked to the Blackstone Edge road and Littleborough by tracks across the field.

Summit Tunnel — the greatest feat of engineering on the line — took three years to build and cost £251,000. After Summit the scenery is typical of the Pennines, with rocky cuttings and twisting streams contrasting with the factories dotted between the towns.

William Cobbett — the radical journalist and author, best known for his *Rural Rides* — wrote: "This part of England is the most interesting that I ever saw.

Here are never-ending chains of hillocks, hill after hill, and hill upon hill, the deep valleys winding about in every direction, and every valley having river or running water.

The view is never the same for two minutes at a time. The buildings are all of solid stone, executed in the best possible manner. Everything appears strong and hard, and made to last forever."

Approaching Todmorden, the Rochdale Canal and the River Calder were crossed by the Gauxholme viaduct, consisting of an iron span over the canal, 17 stone spans of 35 feet, and one of 60 feet over the river. Just beyond this, the canal was crossed again by a very handsome skew bridge with a span of 101 feet; it boasts stone turrets at both ends. The bridge is still standing, although it was reinforced in 1905 to reduce the load on the original girders.

At Todmorden a temporary station was in use until 1844; the present building dates from 1865. At the time the railway arrived, Butterworth described the town as being "an irregularly built place, partly in the bottom of the dale, and partly scattered up and down the opposite side of two hills, in a straggling manner". The population was then about 6,000.

Todmorden station was once connected by a footbridge to the Kings Hotel, where passengers on the Newcastle to Liverpool expresses were served a three-course meal during a lightning stop of just 20 minutes. This practice ended with the provision of dining cars around the turn of the century.

The railway crossed the town on a 55ft viaduct. Three more tunnels followed: Millwood, Castle Hill and Horsfall. Construction problems were encountered beyond Eastwood, where the hill consists of loose sandy earth. A tunnel was begun, but the plan had to be abandoned when the masonry inside the tunnel collapsed. The line was built around the hill, though the tunnel was eventually opened out into a deep cutting between 1846 and 1848. The course of this deviation can still be seen. The new alignment with its reverse curve was always treated with great respect by engine drivers.

The Calder Valley line has witnessed few major accidents, but it was at Charlestown on June 21, 1912 that an express from Manchester to Leeds was derailed, resulting in many deaths.

Next came Hebden Bridge. At the time the railway opened, the population of the town was about 1,500. Butter-

An engine taking on water at Sowerby Bridge station (Jeff Fisher collection)

An L & Y "Highflyer" with a full head of steam at Luddendenfoot (LYR Society Collection)

worth described it as an "extensive but straggling village ". He noted the "several beautiful glens... abounding with picturesque rocks and pleasant knolls, where they who wish to see nothing but nature may feast their eyes to their hearts content". It is still so today.

Mytholmroyd is a Yorkshire name that rolls mellifluously off the tongue. The station is situated on a viaduct, perched high above the town. It is necessary to climb numerous flights of stairs to reach the platform. Branwell Brontë was briefly employed as a ticket inspector at the former station at Luddendenfoot, until it was found that the money he'd taken did not quite tally with the ticket sales.

After Sowerby Bridge tunnel, the original station followed immediately. The station on the present site was partly opened on September 1, 1876 and completed in 1879. Sowerby Bridge was the site of a locomotive shed, becoming a relieving point for the many goods trains which laboured up the gradient to Summit or sought a respite after the long haul from Lancashire.

When the Manchester and Leeds line opened, the station for Halifax was at El-land. The first station was a timber structure, which was replaced by a second station about 200 yards east in 1865. A third station – with a large island platform – was built at a cost of over £11,000 and opened in 1894. Today, passenger trains leave the original route a mile west of Elland, to go via Halifax and Bradford (Exchange) to Leeds.

Next on the original line came Brighouse, described as "one of the most important stations on the line, a tastefully constructed edifice, somewhat in the Chinese style". This was the station for Bradford, then a flourishing and growing town of 45,000 inhabitants, though the station was actually seven miles away by road. Stage coaches would link up with the train arrivals, and take passengers on to Bradford.

Between Elland and Horbury were five low viaducts. At Horbury a short tunnel was dug, but this was opened out in 1903, when the line was widened. Also at Horbury was one of the first works to be started and one of the last to be finished: a cutting three quarters of a mile long and 70 feet deep.

At Wakefield there was a viaduct of

16 arches, filled in to form an embankment when the line was widened to four tracks in 1901. The construction of Wakefield (Kirkgate) station involved the removal of Aspden's Portland Cement Works, the oldest in the world. About 1849, a wagon hoist was installed at the west end of the station to serve a low level yard and a wharf on the Calder.

A mile beyond Wakefield, the Calder was diverted into a new channel to the north of the line to avoid the expense of building two bridges. At Normanton, the Manchester and Leeds joined the North Midland Railway. At the height of its importance, around 60 trains a day called there, exchanging large numbers of passengers and a vast quantity of mail by day and night.

Later, the Scottish expresses called at Normanton to allow the first and second class passengers to dine in the splendid saloons provided on the platforms. These disappeared with the coming of restaurant cars and corridor trains, and only a "refreshment room" was left. That too has now gone.

The Manchester and Leeds Railway opened in stages. On Wednesday July 3, 1839 the first section from Manchester to Littleborough was formally opened. On that great day crowds watched as the first train conveying directors and officers of the company departed from a temporary platform at St George's Street at noon. Pulling the train of 11 carriages were locomotives No. 3 *Stephenson* and No. 2 *Kenya*. A second train followed closely, pulled by locomotives No. 1 *Stanley* and No. 4 *Lancaster*.

Following a stop at Rochdale, the trains continued to the tunnel entrance at Summit, where there were speeches, followed by a collection at Littleborough. On July 4, when the line was opened to the public, 3,100 passengers were carried. The fares from Manchester to Littleborough were 4/- (20p) in 1st class, 2s 6d (13p) in 2nd class and 1s 6d (8p) in 3rd class.

The Normanton to Hebden Bridge section opened on October 5, 1840. As this eastern section of the Manchester and Leeds was still isolated by the un-

Todmorden station on a quiet day in 1900 (Roger Birch collection)

finished Summit tunnel, the North Midland Railway provided the locomotive. It was now possible to travel from Manchester to Leeds, with road coaches connecting Littleborough and Hebden Bridge.

The opening of the eastern section of the line was marked by dangerous behaviour. The Wakefield Journal of October 16, 1840 described how the first train was so full that people rode on the roofs of carriages, standing upright in some cases. Amazingly, nobody was injured.

With the completion of the Summit tunnel the line was finished and opened to the public on Monday March 1, 1841.

At 9.20am a special train left the new station at Oldham Road, carrying the directors, Stephenson and Gooch. At Summit Tunnel the train was joined by a band and proceeded to Normanton, returning to Wakefield for lunch at the station. Here Gooch was presented with £1,000 in appreciation of his work, and he was also given an address and tea service by his staff.

So the line was completed — it had taken four years to build, at a cost of £41,400 per mile. The census of 1831 revealed that the population within ten miles either side of the railway was 1.5 million — one ninth of the country's total population. It was this concentration of people, and of industry, that was to make the Manchester and Leeds one of the most profitable and busy railways in the country.

From Stanhopes to Sprinters – The Calder Valley up to the present day

Travel by the Manchester and Leeds Railway was certainly colourful in those early days. A contemporary report described how "the guards were dressed in flaming red coats" and that some of them carried horns which were worthy of imitation by other companies.

First Class carriages had three compartments. They were upholstered, had sash windows and were painted bright yellow, picked out in black.

Second Class carriages were very similar, also having three compartments. A third type combined a central First Class compartment with two Second Class compartments either side of it.

By contrast, Third Class carriages were open and devoid of seats, with entrances at four corners. They were known as "Stanhopes" after the light, open road vehicles. Wagon passengers — as Third Class travellers were known — were treated as undesirables. They had to report at the booking office at least ten minutes before the train's departure or they would not be booked. Porters were not allowed to carry their luggage.

Thomas Normington, who joined the company in 1847, rose to become Station Master at Oldham and then Superintendent for the Yorkshire district of the Lancashire & Yorkshire railway.

He wrote a book in which he describes travel in those early days.

"I remember going to Manchester to see my grandfather in 1845. I left Thornhill station, which at that time was the only railway station for Dewsbury. I travelled in a passenger wagon train in a stand-up carriage. This carriage was simply a square wood box or wagon, without seats or roof, exposed to all sorts of weather, and the passengers all wedged in, like cattle in a truck.

"Of course, going to see my grandfather, I must go in my Sunday clothes, and had on a new top hat. To my surprise and sorrow, on emerging out of Summit Tunnel, I found my new hat entirely spoilt, the down being frizzled up by the small hot cinders emitted from the funnel of the engine.

"On my return home I again travelled

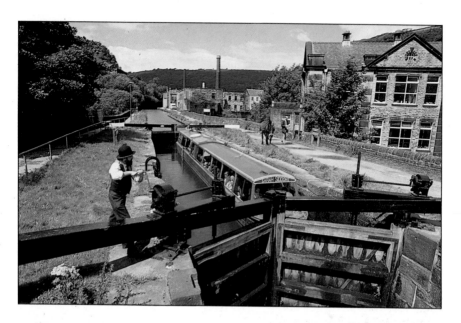

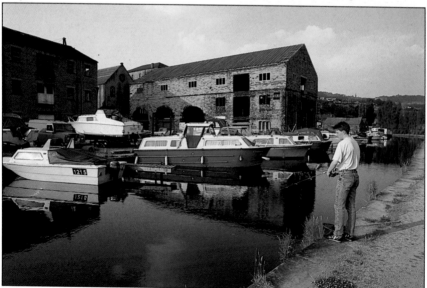

Top: *Now that the Rochdale Canal has been restored to navigable condition, barges once again glide through the water and negotiate the locks. Visitors to Hebden Bridge can enjoy a trip on a horse-drawn narrow-boat.*

Bottom: *Work is under way at Sowerby Bridge to transform the once neglected canal basin into a leisure amenity for the boat users of today. The old warehouses are being renovated, as evocative reminders of the town's industrial past.*

A down stopping train passing Holdsworth Bridge box, near Halifax (Trevor Sutcliffe collection)

by train in a stand-up box in a downpour of rain the whole journey. This and the previous frizzle completely put an end to my brand new hat."

As the M&LR began with coach guards, so it began, like other railways, with coach-style ticket booking. Passengers' names were written twice in a book with counterfoils — along with the date, the destination and the fare. Half the leaf was taken out and given to the passenger, the counterfoil remaining as a record. So booking a train could be a protracted chore.

Then Thomas Edmondson invented a machine for printing railway tickets on cards of standard size, numbered sequentially, and another machine for stamping the date on each one. The Newcastle and Carlisle Railway, for which he worked, was not interested in his invention, but it was taken up by the MLR on which Edmondson became Chief Clerk at Manchester.

The tickets featured the destination, ticket number and date of issue. One side was white, and the other a different colour — depending on the station of issue. Manchester was pink, Mills Hill blue, Rochdale green and Littleborough yellow. Eastbound tickets carried engravings of a fleece, westbound tickets featured a bale of cotton on the back.

The class of ticket was distinguished by a simple form of lines. Third Class were printed with vertical and horizontal lines, Second Class had horizontal lines only, and First Class were plain. This meant that any addition to the ticket only reduced its value. That the system worked was proved on August 20, 1839 when 1,822 people travelled from Manchester — all booked by a single clerk.

In July 1846 the Manchester & Leeds Railway amalgamated with the Manchester, Bolton and Bury Railway. Amalgamations and negotiations spread the company to Preston and Fleetwood, to Liverpool and into other parts of Yorkshire. The company changed its title to one more appropriate to its growing network; in July 1847 it became the "Lancashire & Yorkshire Railway". Before long it was affectionately known, by customers and employees alike, as "the Lanky".

Over the next 30 years or so the L&YR expanded as new main lines, branches and connecting lines were built — including a new through route to Leeds via Halifax and Bradford. It is this route which is taken by today's passenger trains, although British Rail's faster trans-Pennine service goes via Stalybridge and Huddersfield.

While the Manchester and Leeds was a well-engineered line and had introduced a number of innovations, the reputation of the L&YR shrank as rapidly as its operations expanded. Between 1866 and 1880 it paid dividends to shareholders of between five and eight per cent, but it did so at the expense of quality and service.

E L Ahrons, the well known railway author, wrote in the Railway Magazine in 1915: "In the middle of the 1870s it was probably the most degenerate railway in the Kingdom... in spite of the fact that the L&YR was essentially a commercial railway used almost entirely by businessmen and the working classes.... To sum up, the L&YR of 1876 was a railway of ugly, inconvenient stations, of old broken down engines and dirty carriages and of a superlative unpunctuality".

This dreadful state of affairs was not to last. In 1875 a new Chief Locomotive Superintendent, William Barton Wright, was appointed. Over the next ten years he replaced most of the run-down locomotive stock; he is reputed to have scrapped 12 locos at one shed in the first month. His designs were certainly durable and some of his locomotives survived until the 1960s.

By 1910 the L&YR had become one of the best railways in the country, deserving the title of "the business line". Its most important main line was the Calder Valley route. It was a busy railway, with a traffic density greater than any other line. Over its metals — and along the

An L YR Atlantic engine at Halifax, c 1912 (Trevor Sutcliffe collection)

Opposite: *a typical Calderdale scene in Luddenden Dean, with green lanes, dry-stone walls, a mill in the valley bottom and farmhouses up the hillsides.*
Top: *This stone, apparently "balanced" on the slenderest of bases, is part of a formation known as the Bride Stones, situated "on the tops" above Todmorden.*
Bottom: *The view from Ladstone Rock, on the edge of Norland Moor, extends over the valleys of the Ryburn and Calder rivers.*

Calder Valley — was hauled coal from the Lancashire and Yorkshire coalfields to Goole and Liverpool for export, coal to fuel the boilers of the cotton mills of Lancashire and the woollen mills of Yorkshire, woollen traffic to and from the mills, raw cotton from the docks, finished goods, and general merchandise and foodstuffs of all kinds.

The passenger business mainly consisted of people going to and from their places of work, commercial travellers and, of course, excursion traffic to the Lancashire resorts. During the annual Wakes Weeks, whole towns — mills, factories, shops and schools — shut down as people left for the coast.

Excursion and holiday traffic was big business for the Lanky. The first excursion on the Manchester & Leeds had been on Whit Monday 1843, when a 22-carriage train, pulled by two locos, took passengers on the first rail-sea outing. The train ran to Hull, where a connecting steam packet took the excursionists overnight to Edinburgh. They returned on the Wednesday, reaching Manchester late on the Thursday. The cost was £2 2s (£2.10) in First Class, 30/- (£1.50) in Second Class — not bad for four days! In one Whit week, during 1876, no fewer than 1,200,000 passengers were conveyed by the railway.

On the Calder Valley there were changes as the quality of trains improved. Larger locomotives brought increases in speeds and improved reliability. May 1901 saw the introduction of what was to be the crack train on the line — the Fleetwood Boat Express running to and from Bradford and Leeds and connecting with the important Irish steamers.

The L&YR merged with the London & North Western Railway on January 1, 1922, and one year later it became part of the London Midland and Scottish Railway. The next 25 years saw few major changes on the Calder Valley route. Then came nationalisation of the railways in 1948. The first ten years of British Railways hardly affected the line, but then the changes were dramatic. In 1959, diesel multiple trains replaced steam services on the services between Manchester and Rochdale, and the services from Bradford to Huddersfield via Halifax.

In the Beeching era of the 1960s, more stations were closed and more services withdrawn. In one report the Calder Valley was identified as a route to be developed, while the other trans-Pennine line via Huddersfield was to be closed.

A few years later the Calder Valley line was similarly threatened; thankfully, nothing came of these plans, although the Beeching pruning left the Brighouse section of the line unserved by passenger trains. Today it remains the largest town in Yorkshire without a railway station. The West Yorkshire Passenger Transport Executive still nurtures the hope of putting Brighouse and Elland back on the railway map, with a Bradford-Huddersfield service by 1992.

The establishment of Passenger Transport Authorities in West Yorkshire and Greater Manchester has brought improvements in services, modernisation of stations and the welcome re-opening of closed stations during the last 20 years.

The future of the Calder Valley seems assured. It continues to carry freight, and the new trains have increased passenger numbers. The PTEs are encouraging a type of passenger the erstwhile "Lanky" relied on: the excursionists. They can now travel easily to enjoy the pleasures of the wonderful country traversed by the line, while local people can enjoy an improved service to travel to work or for pleasure. ❏

Transport across the Pennines

THE different threads of the transport story in the South Pennines are interwoven — like the road, railway and canal that meander through the hills and valleys. While Pennine wealth was built on the textile industries, it was the transport systems that enabled those industries to thrive.

We should reflect, as we travel the M62 motorway or speed between Halifax and Rochdale on a modern Sprinter train, that trans-Pennine travel was a difficult and hazardous business until comparatively recently. The history of the area has been one of trying to "tame" the wild Pennine landscape, creating routes across the moors and down steep valley-sides to link the emerging centres of the textile industries. Many of the 18 walks in this book follow these old trails and trading routes.

Tracks had been developed between important settlements in pre-Roman times; these routes were improved and consolidated as travel across the Pennines became imperative. While many villages and farmsteads were linked by minor pathways, other tracks were developed as long-distance thoroughfares.

By the 16th century, wheeled traffic was still a rarity. Most goods that needed to be transported were carried by packhorses — often in long "trains" of perhaps 20 or 30 horses. The payloads would be distributed in large pannier bags or sacks, slung over the horses' backs.

Many of the goods were to service the textile trades. Raw materials such as wool and cotton would be brought into the area, and finished pieces of hand-woven cloth would be taken away. But other goods were carried too, as testified by the names still attached to some of these ancient packhorse trails.

Agriculture in the Pennines has always been something of a battle against the elements. Farmers found that the natural acidity of the land required regular spreading with lime. Thus it was that a regular trade in lime spread up between the limestone-rich Bowland district of Lancashire and the South Pennine area. The Limers Gate pack-horse route (part of which is followed in Walk 12) runs along the valley-side of Luddenden Dean and on to Halifax. Salter Rake Gate, which can be traced from Walsden to the village of Lumbutts, is thought to be part of a longer route between the Pennines and the salt-mines in Cheshire.

Some of these ancient packhorse ways now only exist on old maps and in folk memory, but others, happily, can be traced into the valleys and "over the tops" by walkers of today, because they are in the form of paved causeways.

These causeways, very typical of the South Pennines, were made by laying down flagstones, which provided a stable path through the boggiest terrain, and a firm footing for heavily laden packhorses. Their long usage over centuries can be gauged by the deeply hollowed appearance of many causeway stones, due to the passage of countless horses' hooves.

Most of the walks in this book follow sections of paved causeways, or "causeys" as they are known locally. There is something evocative and

Opposite: At Gauxholme, near Todmorden, the road, railway and canal are intertwined in the narrow confines of the valley bottom.
Top: The houses of Calderdale — this one is at Mankinholes — are typically stone-built and sturdy, to withstand the extremes of a Pennine winter.
Bottom: Shibden Hall, near Halifax, is a splendid house dating back to the late 15th century; it was built with money made from the expanding textile trade. Along with the adjacent museum, it is open to the public.

Above: This delightful little packhorse bridge in Pudsey Clough is unusual in being circular in section
Below: Part of a paved packhorse way, called Reddyshore Scout Gate, that descends into the Walsden valley

satisfying about walking these causeways, as we recall the travellers and their horses who laboured along them with goods to sell or barter.

Marker stones and crosses were set up alongside many of these trails. They served to define routes and boundaries, mark points where paths crossed, and some — such as the Allescholes milestone seen on Walk 3 — were inscribed with the mileages to the towns on the route.

The South Pennines are criss-crossed with such causeys. Small becks were forded; larger rivers were spanned by arched stone bridges just wide enough to accommodate a laden pack pony. The old bridge across Hebden Water in Hebden Bridge is a superb example, sited at a strategically important crossing of ancient tracks. A number of these bridges are still standing.

Many of today's roads follow the route of old tracks. Those causeways whose flagstones are undisturbed are often walkable today only because they were too steep to be upgraded into the wider roads required by the waggons and coaches that were much in evidence by the 17th century.

Turnpike Trusts were inaugurated by Acts of Parliament during the early years of the 18th century, with the aim of improving the roads and building new ones where necessary. These trusts kept labourers on the payroll to work on new road-building projects.

The network of Pennine turnpike roads was engineered in the 18th and early 19th centuries by men such as John McAdam and John Metcalfe. The latter was known as "Blind Jack of Knarsborough"; though blind from early childhood, he developed an intimate knowledge of the Yorkshire landscape. It was in 1759 that he constructed the area's first turnpike road — over Standedge, between Marsden and Greenfield.

The Rochdale Canal is spanned at Gauxholme by this splendid railway bridge, complete with castellated towers

Construction of the Rochdale Canal was begun in 1799, under the supervision of the engineer, William Jessop; it was finished just five years later. The speed of construction belied the scale of the operation. The 32 miles of navigable waterway required the building of 92 locks, and more than 100 bridges.

The canal proved to be a very cost-effective method of transporting loads. A canal-boat, pulled by a single horse, could hold a payload equivilent to that carried by as many as 600 pack-horses. Thus it was that both Rochdale and Calderdale were able to exploit to the full the mechanisation of the wool and cotton trades, by transporting both the raw materials and the finished products across the Pennines, to and from ports such as Liverpool and Hull.

The great days of the canal were numbered as soon as the first railway sleepers were laid. Competition from rail and road transport led to a gradual decline in the importance of the Rochdale Canal. The last through trip by a commercial narrowboat from Manchester to Sowerby Bridge was made in 1937. The canal wasn't maintained properly and gradually fell into decline. By 1952 it was effectively closed, with sections silted up and overgrown, and its locks in disrepair.

Happily, the fortunes of the canal took a turn for the better in 1982, when a major project of restoration was begun. Today most of the Rochdale Canal is once again open for traffic, though the barges transport visitors rather than lengths of cloth bound for the sea-ports.

Landscape and Industry

When we look at the South Pennines today, we see a largely man-made landscape — emphasising the dual economy

Opposite: An old cart has been pressed into service as a makeshift gate, above the lovely valley of Luddenden Dean.

Top: Stoodley Pike, built to commemorate victory over Napoleon, is a familiar landmark in Calderdale, and can be seen at some point during most of the walks in this book.

Bottom: The wooded valley of Hardcastle Crags, near Hebden Bridge, is arguably the best-known beauty spot in Calderdale; these stepping stones cross the River Hebden.

that thrived in the area. Farming has always been difficult here due to the climate and the poor quality of the soil. In the past the practice of dividing up farms between all surviving sons led to small-holdings that became increasingly unviable. So it was that many communities combined their farming activities with hand loom weaving. In fact, most upland farms would have been totally uneconomic without this ancilliary income.

Spinning and weaving may have started as side-lines, but they grew in importance. The area soon became known for what was essentially a cottage industry, and improved communications enabled the trade to spread beyond the valleys of the South Pennines. This amalgamation of farming and weaving can be seen in the laithe houses, still to be found on the hillsides, which united farmhouse and barn under the same roof. The barn would house cattle and hay, while weaving would be undertaken in the house.

Cloth halls, where textiles were bought and sold, were established in Heptonstall as early as 1545. The massive Piece Hall in Halifax, built in 1779, shows just how important the woollen trade had become.

The trade flourished, and the population rose accordingly. A reasonable living could be made by many families, despite the harshness of the landscape, but it was the merchants, the "yeomen

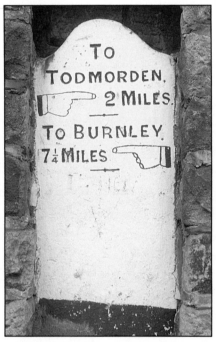

clothiers" who made the fortunes. The merchants would generally supply the raw materials, and the hand-weavers worked on commission.

The merchants built substantial stone houses to match their incomes and aspirations. Known as "Halifax Houses", simply because many are to be found around this pre-eminent textile town, these sturdy halls mark the change of building materials from timber to the gritstone so typical of the South Pennines. The fact that so many of these halls were built is indicative of the wealth accrued from the textile trades. Shibden Hall, visited on Walk 18, is one of the finest — and earliest — examples to be found in the area, being developed from a medieval manor house.

The mechanisation of the textile trade was a gradual affair, as more and more of the processes traditionally done by hand were adapted to machine processes. The flying shuttle, invented in 1733, greatly speeded up the weaving process, though 50 years were to elapse before spinning became mechanised — thanks to Hargreave's "spinning jenny" and Crompton's "mule". Many processes were adapted for use in the homes of the spinners and weavers, though the writing was on the wall for the home-based industries.

As the textile industry became increasingly mechanised, larger premises be-

Left: These characterful mile-posts are a reminder of an age when travel was not as frenetic as it is today. Above: The Steanor Bottom Toll House bears on its façade a replica of the original tolls levied on the various classes of vehicles

came imperative; mills were built in the steep cloughs where water flowed freely to power the machines. The Pennine weavers no longer worked in their homes. They were forced to exchange the independence — and the uncertainties — of self-employment, for long hours and hard labour in the mills. The relationship between boss and worker was an uncompromising one, and the harshness of life for the workers — men, women and even small children — is well documented. Fortunes were made for the few, but at the expense of the many.

As steam took over from water as the most efficient motive power, the mills and the workers moved into the valleys, where bulk supplies of raw materials — such as wool, cotton and coal — could be brought in by canal. Small settlements such as Hebden Bridge, Sowerby Bridge and Todmorden were transformed into major industrial towns, with mills and terraced houses built side by side. The uncontrolled industrialisation, and the appalling conditions in which many people had to live, brought misery to thousands of people.

Conditions improved, as the more en-

31

The Industrial Revolution brought prosperity, and mill-workers, to Hebden Bridge. Terraced houses were built up the hillsides to accommodate them; each house held two families — up and down — and, due to the steeply sloping site, both families had access from street level.

It was a major engineering feat to carve Godley Cutting from the hill above Halifax, to provide a more gentle gradient on the A58

lightened mill-owners and social reformers legislated against some of the worst practices, such as child labour and excessively long hours of work. It is significant, too, that the Co-operative movement, which improved the conditions of workers as both producers and consumers, began in Rochdale and Hebden Bridge.

The industrial revolution changed the South Pennines irrevocably; despite the decline of the textile trade, much of the infrastructure can still be seen today. As we walk the hills and cloughs, we can see the way the landscape has been changed. On the hillsides are the pre-industrial homesteads where weaving and farming were combined. Land was claimed from the moorland, and divided up by well-made stone walls. Old water-powered mills — or their remains — can be seen in the cloughs. The larger, steam-driven mills occupy the valley bottoms; their tall chimneys and "sawtooth" roof-lines are characteristic sights, though smoke billows from few of the chimneys today.

There is much to see, and the walks in this book have been designed to include many of the most interesting features, both natural and man-made. If you want to learn more about the history of the South Pennines, you will find a wide variety of reading material in the Tourist Information Offices listed in the information secton at the back of the book.

❏

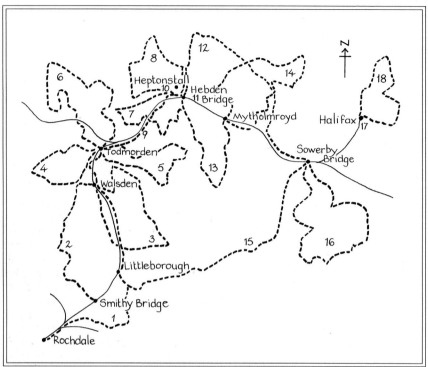

Map by Ruth Abbott

The walks

THE map shows the location of the 18 walks described on the following pages:

1. Hollingworth Lake

*An undemanding 6-mile (11km) walk
between Rochdale and Littleborough,
including Hollingworth Lake — the
"Weavers' Seaport"*

BEFORE starting this walk, you might like to take the opportunity to explore Rochdale's attractive town centre. The magnificent gothic Town Hall is renowned for its stained glass and carvings. It was opened in 1866, by John Bright, the renowned social reformer and radical.

There are also several museums, including the Rochdale Pioneers' Museum - the world's first Co-operative Store - in Toad Lane, and an excellent shopping centre. It is about five minutes on foot from here to the beginning of this walk.

Turn right at the station entrance up the sloping road called High Level, to join the main Oldham road. Cross the road with care and turn right onto an unusual section of elevated pavement, going under the railway and continuing for about a quarter of a mile until you reach the bridge over the Rochdale Canal. Turn left onto the towpath, by a white fence.

This section of the canal is unnavigable, but the towpath provides a pleasant way out of the town centre. You pass an area of factories, mills and yards, which gradually merges into suburbia.

Once you pass beneath the main A664 Rochdale Ring Road bridge, the countryside begins to open out, with views of the Pennines. You pass a swing bridge and a farm on the right, soon going under the railway. Where the canal reaches a blockage at the next main road, cross with care, as this is a three lane expressway leading to the motorway. Continue along the towpath oppo-

site. The canal — now narrower and with scattered trees nearby — leads towards the railway. You pass two stone bridges and, when you are parallel with the railway, you reach a third stone bridge. Go up the stone steps on your left and cross the bridge back over the canal to pass Clegg Farm. Take the track on the left past the derelict Clegg Hall.

This building dates back to 1620, but there were halls on this site as early as 1135. During the first half of the last century, Clegg Hall became a licensed public hall. Known as the "Black Sloven", it was named after the owner's horse.

A number of ghost stories have attached themselves to Clegg Hall. One such tale features an owner of the hall; he was entrusted with the welfare of two orphan children, who were to inherit the estate. In order to gain their inheritance for himself, he threw the luckless pair over the hall's balcony. Because of these crimes the man's soul was not allowed to rest, even after his death. He became a boggart, or evil spirit, and was doomed to haunt Clegg Hall. Whether true or false, such stories made Clegg Hall a place of superstition and notoriety.

Turn right past the buildings and up a cobbled track. Notice the elongated pond on your right. At the end of the lane, cross the road and take the track opposite for 100 yards. Turn left at the footpath sign. From here there is a magnificent view over Rochdale and the Town Hall.

Go past the houses and through a wooden gate at the end of the track, then

This little shop in Toad Lane, Rochdale, was the home of the world-wide Co-operative movement, and is now a museum

follow the stone wall round to the left. Turn right at the gate onto a track and continue over an old cattle grid to follow the waymarked path on the left. This paved path bends up around some trees, known as Bib Knowl plantation. It derives its name from Bible Knoll and was a favourite meeting place for 16th and 17th century religious dissenters. Ignore the stile and continue straight ahead to a wooden kissing gate. From here you can see Hollingworth Lake, built in the early 19th century to provide water for the Rochdale Canal. The 120 acre lake wasn't built in a natural hollow, so high embankments had to be constructed on three sides.

Take the next narrow gap stile on the right, marked by yellow waymarks. This is easy to miss. From here there are even finer views across the Roche valley towards Rochdale and Manchester, and in the other direction across the Pennine moors to Blackstone Edge, with the White House Inn clearly visible.

Go through a wooden gate and along a grassy path. Cross a lane and take the stile on the left along a waymarked path. Follow the path as it bends around a big green knoll called Townough Hill. The path goes through a brown pedestrian gate on the right. From here you can see Rakewood Viaduct carrying the M62 trans-Pennine Motorway across the valley on twenty concrete columns. The motorway was begun in 1966 and opened in 1971.

Go along the board-walk through the willows, which grow on an old lake bed and bogland close to Hollingworth Lake. Take the path ahead by the side of the road, with Hollingworth Lake on your left.

During the 19th century Hollingworth Lake was nicknamed the Weavers' Seaport, because it had much of the atmosphere and amenities of a seaside resort. The lake soon became a popular beauty spot and holiday destination.

The Lancashire & Yorkshire Railway was quick to get on to the bandwagon and soon began promoting excursions to the lake from both Littleborough and Smithy Bridge stations, both only a short walk away. Hotels and refreshment rooms sprang up along the lakeside, and in the heyday of the 1880s Hollingworth Lake offered boats for hire, photographic studios, side-shows, a fairground, fortune tellers, billiards, bowling and a camera obscura. Across the lake, on a small promontory, was the Lake Hotel and pleasure grounds — which could be reached by steamer.

However, by the First World War, Hollingworth Lake's fortunes were on the decline. People were prepared to travel further afield and many of the side-shows and hotels began to look shabby. Though the great Victorian and Edwardian hotels have long gone, you can still take the *Lady Alice* for a boat trip across the lake. Today's visitors are more likely to be found scudding across the water in sailing boats or on wind surfers.

Continue along the lakeside road, via the embankment on the north-east side. Immediately after the end of the embankment, take the approach road (signposted) on the right which leads down to Hollingworth Lake Visitor Centre. Here you'll find an excellent exhibition about Hollingworth Lake and its natural history. There are toilets and a cafe too.

On leaving the visitor centre, continue down in the same direction you have walked, taking the steps on the left up to the path through the woods, before rejoining the road. Go through the gate where the road becomes a track. On the bend take the waymarked path. The paved path swings down to a wooden footbridge. Turn left along the stream where a track joins, and then cross a stream at Lane Foot. Turn left down the track signposted to Littleborough.

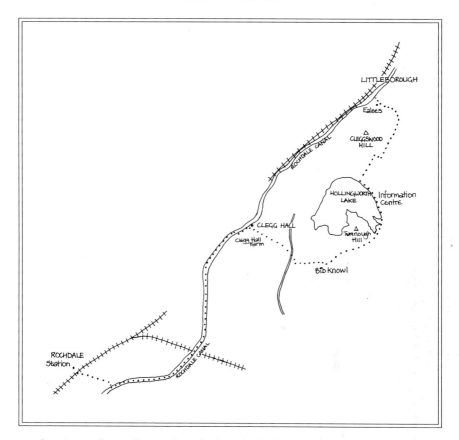

Continue along the track, which winds down the narrow, wooded Ealees valley. There is a badly eroded slope on the left as you turn a corner.

Go past the factory buildings and take the path straight ahead which leads by the back of terraced houses to the canal lock gates. Go down the canal towpath which emerges onto a road. Continue in the same direction; after about 50 yards take the subway on the right into Littleborough station. ❑

Left: Hollingworth Lake, near Littleborough, is popular with people who enjoy'"messing about in boats"

2. Walsden to Smithy Bridge

*A 9-mile (16km) walk over the Long Cause-
way — an old packhorse route — past a
submerged Pennine village*

FROM the newly reopened station at Walsden, walk right along the main road in the direction of Rochdale. Turn right immediately after Trinity Methodist Church, up Inchfield Road — a lane that climbs steeply up the valley-side. As the gradient levels off a little, you will find a bench where you can sit and enjoy the view up the valley towards Gauxholme and Todmorden.

Carry on up the road until it becomes a rough farm track, and goes over a cattle grid towards a farm ahead. This track is Brown's Road, known as Dick Cote in the days when it was a resting place for packhorse men and their teams. When you reach the farm, take the gate on your left to follow a green track down to a stile.

Cross the stile and descend into Ramsden Clough to Ragby bridge, an old packhorse bridge. Continue up the other side, following the wire fence. Go over the stile on the right-hand side of the gate to join a farm track, before going through a gate on the right. Follow the wall, passing under the pylons, and ignoring the green track that swings off to the right. From here you can see Cranberry Dam with the moors behind rising up to Blackstone Edge.

Continue uphill, following a wall to your left. Towards the summit there are long stretches of paved causeway climbing up over the hill. This is Long Causeway, a packhorse route from Burnley to Halifax, which runs along the northern rim of Calderdale. The route is most strongly associated with the monks of Whalley Abbey and the de Lacy family of Clitheroe; both had widely dispersed land holdings in the area.

During the Middle Ages the woollen industry grew increasingly important, and a flourishing trade developed in transporting wool to the small Pennine weaving settlements and then taking the finished products to the cloth halls of Halifax, Heptonstall and elsewhere. Galloway ponies were often used for this porterage, and parts of Long Causeway were, until recently, known as Galloway Road or Galloway Gate.

The combination of peaty soil and heavy rainfall often made the going difficult for laden pack-ponies. So it was that on major routes like the Long Causeway, flagstones or "causey stones" were laid to give the ponies a firmer footing. This is still the most effective solution to the problem of footpath or bridleway erosion !

Over the brow of the hill is the great sweep of the Lancashire plain. On a clear day you can sometimes see as far as the huge radio telescope at Jodrell Bank. Directly below you is Watergrove Reservoir. The path at this point seems almost to peter out, but if you look carefully you can see it swing left, down the hillside and towards the reservoir.

In this area you will see the spoil heaps from the old drift mines. The coal seams were no more than a foot thick and produced poor quality coal, so extraction was only on a small scale for domestic fires and local steam-powered mills.

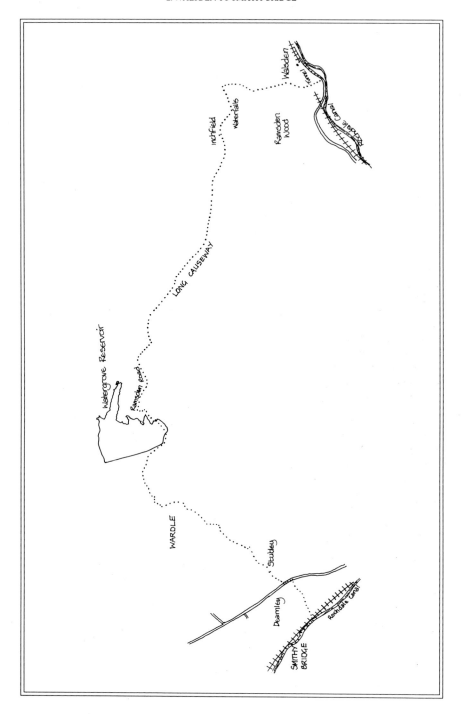

Make for a walled track marked by two gate-posts. Follow the track past the preserved ruins of the cottages of Little Town down to the reservoir. Watergrove Reservoir was constructed in 1930; the village of Watergrove was flooded in the process. Beneath the water is the site of what was once a thriving community of 200 people. It consisted of over 40 houses, two pubs, a chapel, a smithy and two mills.

The village and surrounding upland farms were cleared to make way for the reservoir, which was needed to provide water for Rochdale. Watergrove Reservoir is now a popular destination for fishermen and wind-surfers; there is a Warden Centre and toilets near the landing area.

A detour is necessary here, because the stones of Long Causeway disappear under the waters of the reservoir and reappear at the other side. Turn left to follow the track around the reservoir, past the remarkable and poignant "Wall of History". Set into the reservoir wall are a number of date stones (the oldest inscribed 1646), lintels from old mullioned windows, and a drinking trough rescued from Watergrove village. A massive stone plaque inscribed "Watergrove Mill 1888" is the only surviving relic of the village's cotton mill.

Continue to the car park below the dam. Walk through the car park and swing left to follow the cobbled setts down into Wardle. You will find a typical Pennine mill town with grey stone

Opposite: The flagged path known as Long Causeway provides an unmistakable route over the moors to Watergrove Reservoir
Below: The "Wall of History" at Watergrove Reservoir incorporates mullion windows, datestones and other interesting items

houses, mills and an imposing Methodist Chapel overlooking the main square. If time is not pressing, have a look at the 19th century church with its unusual east window depicting 16 scenes from the life of Christ.

Opposite the church, look for a footpath sign on the left between two houses. Go through the alleyway or ginnel between the gardens and over the little bridge to a stone kissing gate, keeping the vaccary stones on your right. Vaccary stones, typical of this part of Lancashire, are great slabs of stone set on end in the ground to serve as field enclosures for dairy cattle.

Go through a small gate, past Bank Barn Cottages and turn right down the track. Follow it until you approach a set of white gate-posts where the track swings sharply to the right. Turn right and continue for a few yards, but look for a footpath sign and stile on the right. Cross the stile and continue up the stone steps ahead for a short distance, before taking the wooden stile on the left.

Straight ahead you can see Hollingworth Lake.

Follow the path, contouring round the hillside to a stile. Ahead is Birch Hill Hospital, once a Victorian workhouse, but now a hospital serving the Rochdale area. Descend to a rough track below, bearing left through a hollow to a wooden stile; continue along the track ahead. The track bears right, passing behind a new housing estate on the left before emerging at the main Littleborough-Rochdale road.

Cross the road to the handsome 16th century Stubley Old Hall, which is now a restaurant. Turn left past the hall and a short row of terraced houses; turn right immediately after them to go down the track. Follow it until it bears right; your route is straight ahead.

Continue along the path over a footbridge towards a flight of steps; these lead under the railway to rejoin the canal towpath. Turn right and follow the canal, which leads directly to Smithy Bridge station. ❏

3. Reddyshore Scout and the Reservoirs

A 7-mile (13km) walk that follows an old packhorse way along the top of the Walsden valley

FROM Walsden station walk left along the main road until you reach the Waggon and Horses pub. Take an enclosed path that starts behind the pub, and climbs quite steeply to the left up the hillside. When you meet a minor road, cross over and continue up the cobbled path in front of you. Soon you meet the road again; follow it to the left as it climbs, giving extensive views over Walsden and the valley.

You pass two farms — Lower and Upper Allescholes Farms — as the road clings precariously to the very edge of the ridge. As foreign as it sounds, "Allescholes" is from old English and means "the hut of the alders". The name reminds us that at one time many of these Pennine hills were well wooded. Deforestation has been almost total, and the few wooded cloughs that remain are starting to be seen as landscape features worth preserving. New tree-planting schemes are also progressing.

Once you pass Moor Hey Farm, the road deteriorates into an unmade track. You are now walking the famous old packhorse route of Reddyshore Scout Gate: the oldest route along the valley. This is good easy walking — with the valley falling away steeply to your left, and with moorland and sheep for company to the right.

Go through a gate; 200 yards past it, look out on your left for a real antiquity. The Allescholes milestone is a small (only about 2ft high) squared-off stone, all four sides bearing the distances — al-beit rather optimistic ones — to four towns: Rochdale 5, Burnley 9, Halifax 10, Todmorden 2. The stone marks the junction of two important packhorse routes; you can look down to the left to see a track heading into the valley towards Walsden, and eventually to Halifax.

Your route, however, is straight on along the ridge-top track. As you proceed, you will see that sections of the track are paved. It's a shame that so much builders' rubble has been tipped here, just before you walk beneath the crackling wires of the National Grid, suspended between huge pylons.

Down to the left are the houses of Warland, with a little wooded clough behind. Notice some of the walling on the left of the track, that has, over the centuries, kept this route stable and level, despite the steepness of the slope that falls away to the left.

You are almost walking above the route of the railway as it goes through the Summit tunnel. The tunnel is 2,885 yards long, and as much as 100 yards beneath the surface. Opened in 1840, the tunnel was the cause of death for a number of the men who laboured to build it.

The route of the tunnel is marked on the hillside beneath you by air-shafts, the first of which soon appears. In the valley below is the Bird i' th' Hand pub, an inn built in 1825 to exploit the traffic using the turnpike road that had been opened just four years earlier.

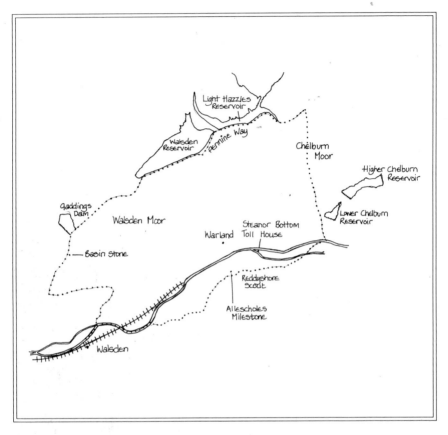

Through a couple of gates you can now see Upper Chelburn Reservoir across the valley; you will be getting a closer view of it before the end of the walk. You now begin a gradual descent, that still follows the edge of the ridge. Another landmark now comes into view, down in the valley bottom: Steanor Bottom Toll House.

After a farm track joins your route from the right, you find yourself on a well-preserved section of paved causeway — though all too soon the stones disappear beneath tarmac. Now you cross Owler Clough and its unassuming little stream. Here is another good example of walling to keep a level track over the dip. You see more air-shafts down to the left; you can admire their brick construction as you walk across the line of the tunnel.

After a gate you meet a road; cross it and take the waymarked footpath ahead. It takes you straight down into the valley, towards an old quarry on the opposite side. You meet the main road conveniently close to the Summit Inn, which might provide a timely lunch stop.

Your path continues just to the left of the pub, down a little cobbled track. Cross the bridge over the canal, and follow a track ahead for about 50 yards. Then go left up to a wooden footbridge over an outflow channel that takes water from the adjacent reservoirs into the canal. The footbridge, and the gravelled path leading from it, has been developed by the Oldham and Rochdale Groundwork Trust (and other bodies too) as the Summit Trail.

Follow this path through a gate marked NWWA (North West Water Authority). Walk about 50 yards and then bear left, uphill, and away from Lower Chelburn Reservoir. Your path takes in a couple of hairpin bends, which lessen the gradient, and then heads across the moorland. The path is indis-

of the beck; a few yards further on is a small footbridge comprising just a few wooden planks. You are now heading across lonely Chelburn Moor. Ahead are rocky outcrops; just before you reach them, you meet a broad sandy track heading to left and right. This is part of the Pennine Way.

Turn left along the level track, with Head Drain accompanying it on the right. After a few yards you will see old quarry workings to the right, and get

As the road climbs up to join the Reddyshore Scout Gate packhorse way, there are fine views back over Walsden

tinct in places; if you are doubtful, just head to where a line of electricity pylons disappears over the horizon.

You can now see both Upper and Lower Chelburn Reservoirs to the right. Cross a little arched footbridge over one of the becks that feeds into the reservoirs. Pass a little dammed-off section

extensive views to the left over Littleborough and Rochdale. Keep left at a junction of tracks, beneath the line of pylons overhead.

Now you walk along the edge of Light Hazzles Reservoir, after which another reservoir is approached; this is a much larger body of water called Warland

The Allescholes Milestone: a splendid landmark that provides the mileage to Halifax, Burnley, Rochdale and Todmorden

The Basin Stone, with its 'fish-tail' profile, was once used as an open-air pulpit by travelling Methodist ministers

Reservoir. Keep to the left of this reservoir; at the far end you cross a little bridge by a "Danger, No Swimming" sign. Take a lesser path to the left, just after the bridge. Soon you will be able to pick up a path that bears to the right across the moor. In places the path is elusive; just try to keep a level track, parallel with the Walsden valley on your left.

This is a stony landscape of bracken and cotton grass. Your next landmark is a small reservoir called Gaddings Dam: an isolated stretch of water. Turn left at the end of the dam and follow a more obvious path downhill. Make a little detour off the track, shortly, to investigate the Basin Stone — an oddly-shaped outcrop which, from one angle at least, resembles a fish-tail. This prominent landmark was one of the many sites used by peripatetic Methodist preachers to deliver their open-air sermons.

Carry on walking down the sandy track; 150 yards past the Basin Stone is a marker stone to the right, with the letter "L" engraved upon it. The path heads towards a wooded clough. When you reach a track, go left along it, back down the Walsden valley, with Walsden itself slightly to your right.

You soon find a paved causeway beneath your feet, which makes a delightful way to finish off the walk. It's very evocative to walk this well-worn causeway, just as the pack-ponies once did. In

A well-preserved section of paved causeway completes this walk, as you make the descent back into Walsden

places you can see that the line of paved stones has been augmented by smaller stones set down on both sides. The causeway is soon accompanied by a wall on the right.

You may have to pick your way through a few yards of the causeway that have become boggy, even in high summer. You approach a house, go through a gate, and keep ahead along an enclosed track. Look out for the old-fashioned red telephone box in the gar-

den of this house.

You soon join a tarmac road, to head downhill past more houses, and directly towards Walsden.

When you see a sign announcing that this is Hollingworth Lane, the road bears right — but you can take a delightful cobbled path ahead. Cross the canal by Travis Mill Lock, and walk right along the main road back to Walsden railway station. ❑

4. Gorpley Clough from Todmorden

A 6-mile (11km) moorland ramble which includes a fine wooded clough and an example of old road building

THE civic pride enshrined in these little Pennine towns could have no more grandiose expression than in the town hall. It was built in an unconstrained classical Greek style. Here, in the middle of Todmorden, is a veritable Greek temple, topped by statues of female figures on a dais incribed with Yorkshire and Lancashire, for the building actually sits astride what was once the county boundary.

This is appropriate, because Todmorden, although sited in West Yorkshire, traditionally had as much in common with the cotton towns of Lancashire.

Walk along the Rochdale road for about a quarter of a mile. Turn right between terraced houses, up an unmade track called Dobroyd Road. You may also notice a stencilled "Calderdale Way" logo and a yellow arrow.

The track soon crosses the canal, and then the railway line; take care to look and listen for trains approaching. Bear left uphill, along a shady track. You now begin to get a bird's-eye view over Gauxholme, its railway bridge and canal. When you come out at a little crossroads, go straight ahead uphill; this is Stones Road. Keep walking until the road makes a very tight hairpin bend to the right. Go left through a gap stile at

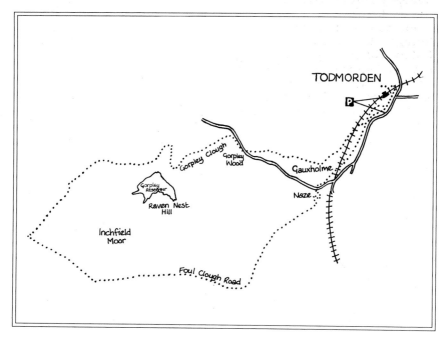

the elbow of the bend, and climb steeply to the right. A few well-placed stone steps will aid your progress.

At the top you come out onto another little crossroads of paths. Bear sharp right here; a very pleasant path climbs between walls, giving terrific views both up and down the Calder valley. The path soon becomes an excellently preserved paved causeway. Pass a caravan park, below and to your left, as you rapidly leave the Calder valley behind to climb above the Burnley road. Join a track and keep going uphill until you see, on the left, a field gate and kissing gate side by side.

Go through the gate and walk downhill towards a splendid example of a laith farmhouse, with barn and living accommodation beneath the same roofline. Before you reach the building, go right along an enclosed path. This pleasant path soon descends towards a mill with prominent chimney. When the walls end you carry on, slightly to the right; head for the top of a small wood. Enter the wood via an iron kissing gate. The path crosses a tiny stream and then takes you gradually downhill and onto the main Burnley road.

Go right here for about 300 yards, and then take a path on the opposite side of the road: a newly refurbished route which takes you through the woodland of Gorpley Clough. The path is rather artificial in places, perhaps more suited to a suburban garden than open woodland. Yet it does make for easy walking, with footbridges and steps to guide your feet and take you across any boggy bits.

The path takes you past a couple of waterfalls, which make a pretty sight

Opposite: The mill towns of the South Pennines vied with one another to produce the most splendid town hall. This "Greek" extravaganza is in Todmorden.
Below: The first section of this walk offers extensive views down over the terraced houses of Gauxholme and to the fells beyond

after rain. You climb up steps, past an incongruously sited privy, into the workings of Gorpley Reservoir. Bear right, along a gravel road that takes you around the buildings and up to where the route forks. Go left here, beneath tall electricity pylons that stretch across the fells.

Bear right at a house, to go uphill along a slightly sunken track. From here you get good views down over Gorpley Reservoir. When the track veers left into a field, carry straight on to maintain the same height. Keep close to a wall on your left, cross a couple of stiles, and head for the end of the clough. The path is not very distinct here; if in doubt, just try to maintain the same height.

Once you round the end of the clough, bear slightly to the right across the tussocky grass of open moorland, until you reach a wall. Go left along the wall as it stretches dead ahead of you and over the horizon. Once you reach that horizon, you get panoramic views down into the valley which encloses Todmorden and towards Ramsden Wood on the right.

Keep straight ahead, walking downhill by the wall. When the wall ends, continue in the same direction, to pass once again beneath the wires strung between the giant electricity pylons. Join the sandy road you see ahead; this is Foul Clough Road. Follow this track until you arrive at a little pond much frequented by thirsty cows. Take a track that heads off left just before the pond. After about 100 yards, the track becomes a fine paved causeway.

On approaching a wall, and another track coming in from the right, bear right to accompany the wall and soon go through a gate. Walk down an enclosed

Below: An old gatepost provides a foreground to the still water of Gorpley Reservoir
Opposite: The view from the Naze, a steep old road that winds down from Inchfield Pasture into Gauxholme

track until you find yourself on an old and superbly engineered track, known as the Naze.

Follow this cobbled way and enjoy the views over Gauxholme — where road, railway and canal are squeezed into the narrow confines of the valley floor — and Todmorden beyond.

The Naze needs a few hairpin bends to render the gradient passable by pack-horse traffic. Even so it remains a steep descent, a fact which has saved this route from ever being improved and tarmaced over.

From Gauxholme you can avoid walking along the road by taking the canal towpath back into Todmorden. There are locks to admire, and the "Great Wall of Todmorden" — a huge retaining wall close to the centre of town. ❏

5. Stoodley Pike from Todmorden

A breezy 8-mile (15km) walk along Langfield Edge to investigate a monument that commemorates victory over Napoleon

FROM Todmorden station, make your way down to the roundabout by the Town Hall. Go right along the Rochdale road, and cross the canal. On the left is the Golden Lion pub. It was here, on an evening in 1814, that a patriotic trio met; now that the Napoleonic War was over they wanted to commemorate the peace with a suitably grand monument.

The gesture was no doubt prompted by commercial, as well as nationalistic, instincts, because the war had seriously curtailed the export of cloth on which Calderdale's fortunes were based.

The result was Stoodley Pike: a splendidly phallic structure that is the destination for this walk. The site, atop Langfield Edge, was an inspired choice for a monument. At a height of 1,310 feet above sea level, Stoodley Pike is visible for miles around — certainly at some point during most of the walks in this book. You cross a ridge, or turn a corner, and it will suddenly appear on the horizon like an admonishing finger.

Turn left immediately after the Golden Lion pub, and walk up the road. Take the first road on the left, to avoid getting lost in a housing estate. At the top of the hill the road soon peters out at Longfield Terrace. Here take a track to the left, to find yourself suddenly "on the tops", with good views back over Todmorden.

When the track forks, keep left by a "public footpath" sign to a farm building. From here you will get the first glimpse of Stoodley Pike on the horizon ahead. Pass farm buildings, and carry on along the farm track to a road. Go left to find a pub, the Shepherds Rest, in splendid isolation. The position may be windswept, but the welcome is warm.

Opposite the pub is a track leading through a gate onto Langfield Common. The sign reads "Gaddings 1, Pennine Way 2". From here you can look down into the valley towards Mankinholes and Lumbutts — its giant triple-decker water wheel tower being particularly prominent. You will find, as you walk, that Stoodley Pike appears distant almost until you reach it: a rather odd phenomenon.

Through the gate, take the obvious path ahead, uphill. At the remains of some old quarry workings, the track forks. Take the left-hand track, round the shoulder of Langfield Edge; it soon narrows to a path. This route has been expertly engineered in parts to provide good level walking despite the steep slope. You walk beneath rocky escarpments as you gain height.

Once you round the head of the clough, you start to walk directly towards Stoodley Pike. The track descends soon after, but you take instead a lesser path, slightly to the right, which offers bright and breezy walking over bouncy cotton grass. As you pick your way through an area of rocks, you will see Withens Clough Reservoir on the right.

Your path ahead is unmistakable; you follow the ridge top with an extensive panorama spread out to your left. Soon there is a meeting of the ways, at Withins Gate, close by a marker stone known as Long Stoop. A signpost reaffirms that

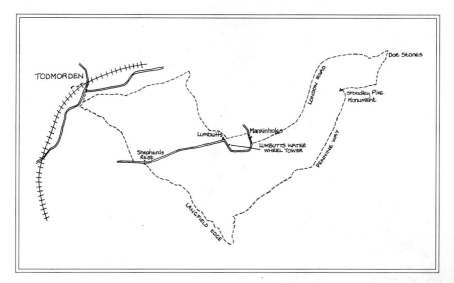

here you are walking a section of the Pennine Way. A beautifully constructed paved causeway crosses your route at right angles. The Calderdale Way follows it, and the causeway is also used by Pennine Way walkers to gain access to the youth hostel at Mankinholes — surprisingly the only one within the part of Calderdale covered by this book.

The Pennine Way logo, used for waymarking purposes, is an acorn: an appropriate device considering how many other long-distance footpaths have been inaugurated since the Pennine Way became Britain's first.

You can enjoy excellent level walking along the ridge, on a clearly defined path; eventually Stoodley Pike will be reached, and you can escape from the wind in the lea of this splendid Victorian monument.

The monument you can see today is actually Mark II. The first version, built to quite a different design, was undone by the extremes of Pennine weather and collapsed in 1854, at the onset of the Crimean War. When peace came two years later, another meeting was held at the Golden Lion pub in Todmorden. A public subscription provided the funds for Stoodley Pike to be rebuilt in the form you can see today.

There are stairs inside the monument — though you would need a torch to climb them — up to a viewing platform a good way up the full height of 120 feet.

Head away from Stoodley Pike, and the valley it overlooks, to keep on a path (still the Pennine Way) that soon passes a drinking trough inscribed "Public Slake Trough". Negotiate a gap-stile in a wall and, immediately after, a ladder-stile on the left over an adjacent wall. The Doe Stones can be seen to your right, as the path descends. Ahead of you, across the valley, is the hill-top village of Heptonstall, with its church tower head and shoulders above the houses.

At a signpost you leave the Pennine Way. Follow a wide track to the left; it takes you back almost in the direction of Stoodley Pike before swinging to the right on a level way. This is an old route called London Road, a good track for

---

Overleaf: A solitary walker strides up the beautifully paved causeway that leads from Mankinholes over Withins Gate

striding out. It offers a gentle descent past farms, and is enclosed between walls in the section before Mankinholes. You will notice that the enclosed part of the track is at least 20 feet wide.

Mankinholes is a tranquil little hamlet today, though the extended horse troughs at the roadside recall the days when teams of pack-ponies came this way. Look out, too, for a number of stone mounting blocks. There are several splendid old houses in the village, including the youth hostel with its mullioned windows.

About a hundred yards beyond the village you come to a house adjacent to a Methodist burial ground. On the opposite side of the road is a paved enclosed path, waymarked "Calderdale Way", which brings you out just by the Top Brink pub in Lumbutts, at one time a packhorse inn.

You will try the door in vain, however, if you arrive at lunchtime during the week, as midday openings are normally only at weekends.

The pub overlooks the cluster of houses that constitutes Lumbutts, a little hamlet dominated visually by a huge water tower — all that now remains of Lumbutts Mill.

The tower represents an ingenious

A memorial obelisk in the Methodist burial ground at Mankinholes echoes the shape of Stoodley Pike on the fell beyond

method of utilising the motive power of water. In the tower — all of 100 feet high — three enormous water wheels were mounted one on top of another. Each overshot wheel was 30 feet in diameter and six feet wide.

Water was directed over them via a complex series of mill races on different levels, from the four dams which can still be seen nearby. The adjacent site is currently being developed as an outdoor pursuits centre.

If you want to take a closer look at the water tower, there are steps straight down from the pub. To continue on the walk, climb the steps back to the pub, and go left to take a path that weaves between a house and garage. You soon arrive in a field; your way ahead is — albeit briefly — a section of causeway. Bear half left at a gate and then follow the wall on your right — slightly downhill and towards a wooded clough.

Negotiate a gap-stile in a wall and then head slightly uphill across a field to meet another gap in the wall ahead. From here you can look down into the valley towards Todmorden. Your path — better defined now and paved in parts — leads ahead, downhill, as the valley sides become ever steeper. Soon you are accompanying a chain-link fence to the left: on the opposite side of the fence is what a sign announces to be a landfill site: in other words a rubbish dump. You reach a farm track shortly, and then join a road by a cluster of cottages. Turn to the right down the road until you meet the Rochdale Canal. The easiest way back into Todmorden is to cross the canal and walk left along the towpath. ❏

Left: A setted path leads down to Lumbutts Water Tower, which housed no less than three water wheels, mounted vertically

6. On the Tops from Todmorden

An exhilarating 7-mile (13km) ramble which includes splendid views, interesting rock formations and a well-preserved causeway

FROM Todmorden station walk downhill for a few yards, and then turn left along a road that goes beneath the railway. Climb the steep set of steps (Ridge Steps) you see ahead of you. Turn right at the top of the steps and, when you have a choice of two tracks to take, choose the left-hand one. It will take you slightly uphill and give good views back over Todmorden and, in the foreground, a park and cricket ground. The path weaves through pleasant woodland.

When you reach a tarmac road go right, downhill, to meet the main Burnley road. Cross the road and walk left along it. After 500 yards go right along Stoney Royd Lane, which is waymarked "Calderdale Way". When the road comes to an end at the drive of a large house, you bear right along a track. Soon the track forks; the right track goes beneath the railway, but you take the track to the left which narrows to a path.

Carry straight on as the path leads onto a tarmac road. Follow the road uphill as it deteriorates into a stony track. At the top of a hill you come to a T-junction of tracks. To the left is a track leading down into Lydgate; you take the right option, with the first few yards paved with a double set of flagstones.

The track winds up through Kitson Woods, with Cat Hole Clough to your left. You will soon see the unruly pile of Orchan Rocks ahead of you. From here you can look back over Todmorden and, to the left, as far as Stoodley Pike. The path continues to the left of the rocks, along the shoulder of the hill, as Cat Hole Clough comes to an end at Hudson Bridge, a tiny bridge over an equally tiny beck. To the left is Hartley Royd Farm; to the right, on the horizon, are the Hawks Stones.

When you reach Hartley Royd Farm, walk straight through the farmyard between the house and the outbuildings. Go through the gate ahead of you to take an enclosed track. After a cattle grid, follow the track as it hugs the wall to your left and passes a tall mast.

The track continues, with wonderful views opening up to both left and right. Keep left, to walk along the ridge-top looking down into Cat Hole Clough. The path narrows, but is still easy to follow. As you enter woodland, the drop becomes precipitous on your left — so watch your step. To judge from the walling that helps to keep the track level despite the steep slope, this was once a more important route than it is today.

Soon you round two steep and acute bends. Then go slightly downhill as the path forks, to enjoy extensive views down to the left into Lydgate and Todmorden beyond. It is during the next section of this walk that you can see most clearly the riven cloughs, the steep-sided valleys, the farms "on the tops", and the mills and communities in the valley bottoms. At every turn the landscape seems to change.

Follow this pleasant track, which goes around the shoulder of the hill, among scattered trees, bracken and grasses. Soon you find yourself walking towards Cornholme — half hidden in the folds of the hills — as this side of the valley now hoves into view. When the track forks

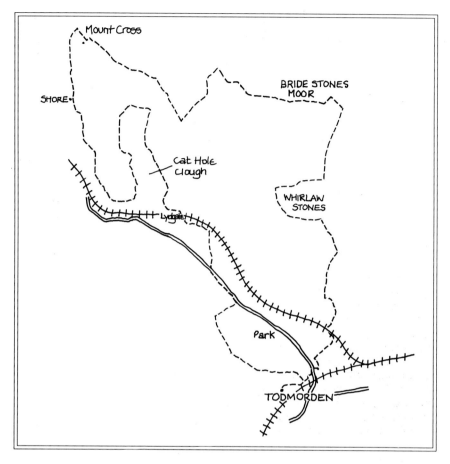

again, keep right, to head slightly downhill towards Cornholme.

Just past a ruined barn, bear slightly right, uphill, to locate a stile across the fence ahead. You have level walking, until you come up against a cobbled path which runs along the edge of a wooded clough.

Turn right, quite steeply uphill, to follow this cobbled way. The track bears left at the top to keep going around the woodland. After a few more yards you cross a little beck, bisect a pair of gateposts and then — as rather a surprise in the middle of a wood — you are confronted by a flight of stone steps, of some

age, complete with iron hand-rail. When you reach the top of the steps, their presence becomes less of a mystery, for you emerge to find Shore General Baptist Chapel — and graveyard — currently in a sad state of disrepair.

You now enter the little hamlet of Shore; go past the small, uncluttered collection of farms and houses to a little T-junction of minor roads. Walk right, up the road. It's steep and twisty, but after less than half a mile you bear right, opposite Lower Mount Farm, on an enclosed track.

After a few yards you will see Mount Cross on the left: a stone edifice of unde-

Sturdy dry-stone walls, typical of Calderdale, are topped by the outcrop of Orchan Rocks

niably great age but of uncertain provenance. It is sited on the junction of important packhorse routes, and may have been built by the monks of Whalley Abbey to guide travellers passing this way.

Carry on, keeping to the left of Lower Intake Farm, along a narrow path. This is good level walking, with extensive views to the right. Keep on this pleasant enclosed track, through three gates, then go through a stile next to a gate in the beautifully made stone wall on the left. Follow the tractor track uphill towards the rocks on the skyline. Pass between two farms and up to the left end of the escarpment of rocks. Look left at this point and you will see, just five minutes' walk away, a white pub — the Sportsman's Arms, which is worth a detour if the thirst is upon you.

Otherwise your route is along the ridge to the right, investigating the rocks

as you go. Many have been weathered into interesting shapes which seem to metamorphose into recognisable objects and creatures as you walk. These are the Bride Stones. Towards the end of the group of stones is the highest point, topped by a triangulation point. A few yards further on you will discover quite an oddity: a big ovoid rock that appears to defy gravity by being supported on the slenderest of bases.

This strangely weather-worn rock may give a clue as to how the Bride Stones got their name. At one time, apparently, there were two such "balancing" stones, known as the "Bride" and "Groom", until one of the stones was pushed over.

Having investigated the Bride Stones, carry on in much the same direction, along an ill-defined path, until you meet a road. Turn right here and, after 100 yards, turn right down another road towards a tall radio mast. Pass the mast and go over the crest of the hill, to get a grand view into the valley.

In these fields of tussocky grass you may see birds such as Skylarks, Meadow Pipits and Wheatears. The Wheatear is a small bird, of the thrush family, which is immediately recognisable by the flash of white rump as it flies. This gives the bird its name: a corruption of the very literal name of "white arse".

Pass Windy Harbour

Farm; the road peters out shortly after. Take an enclosed path to the right; you enter open pasture and bear slightly to the left to arrive at another pile of rocks, Whirlaw Stones — a fine place to sit and enjoy the view over Todmorden.

Just beneath the stones you will find a beautifully engineered paved causeway which here is part of the Calderdale Way. Join the causeway as it goes left. Notice how seamlessly the stones fit together,

Mount Cross, situated at a junction of old tracks, provides the turning point for this walk

From the Bride Stones can be seen lonely farmhouses facing out onto the fells

and how worn they have become through centuries of use.

The causeway ends abruptly at a field-gate; carry straight on as the track runs between walls. You are soon back into open pasture by a farm, after which the track forks. Take the track to the right; it soon widens and goes through wood-land with a steep drop to the right. Descend to a little crossing of tracks, by a farm. Take the right-hand route downhill.

The track makes a serpentine descent to a collection of houses, where it becomes a tarmac road. Carry on downhill and back into Todmorden. ❑

Right: The latter stage of this walk passes Whirlaw Rocks and follows this section of paved causeway

7. Jumble Hole Clough

A 6-mile (10km) walk from Hebden Bridge to explore two delightful wooded cloughs, on either side of the Calder valley

LEAVE Hebden Bridge station, and go immediately right, to continue past the station building and then underneath the railway line. Walk uphill on the rough tarmac road; turn right, uphill, just before some new houses. This is Palace House Road.

After about 300 yards is a two-car garage on the left; a few yards further on is a gap and steps, also on the left. Keep a look out because these steps are easy to miss. Take this narrow path that goes up between garden walls until you reach a wider path at the top. Go right here, to walk at the back of houses. After 150 yards you meet another track, which bears left, uphill, between walls. After another 150 yards, bear acutely right, as the track leads through woodland. All these twists and turns are merely to avoid a steep climb directly up the valley side.

At the next dog-leg corner, you go left up a slightly sunken way which becomes an enclosed path betweeen walls. Soon the path goes under a road, via an arched tunnel. Continue up the walled track, till you reach a little crossing of tracks. Keep straight on until you reach a gate and, a few yards further on, a tarmac road. Go right along this road; after 150 yards take a farm track to the left, way-marked "Stoodley". This track passes a farm on its way to a wooden stile.

Cross the stile and walk just to the right of a wooded area between walls, which descends into the clough. You soon cross an old bridge over a little beck, and follow the path uphill and to the right, until you meet an unmade track. Follow this track to the right; it accompanies the clough downhill. At this point you have once again joined the Pennine Way. The track weaves pleasantly through woodland and down into the valley bottom.

Cross the Rochdale Canal and go right at the main road. After 50 yards take a path on the left. It is called Underbank Avenue, as well as being waymarked "Pennine Way". Go through a short tunnel beneath the railway. The Pennine Way goes straight up an enclosed cobbled path ahead of you. It's a bit steep, but no matter, because you take the easier option: bear left as soon as you are through the tunnel under the railway, to meander through a collection of houses.

Soon you will see another short tunnel under the railway line; here you bear right, immediately after a couple of bungalows. This unmade track bears a sign, "Private Road", but is nevertheless a right of way for walkers. Pass some old cottages and Spa Mill to enter the intimate surroundings of Jumble Hole Clough. This delightful clough is where local people go for a bit of peace and quiet, on those days when Hardcastle Crags are chock-full of visitors.

Walk up through woodland, passing remains of other old mill buildings — all long since abandoned and going inexorably "back to nature". Notice, too, the various weirs, dams and outfalls that once helped the beck to power the mills

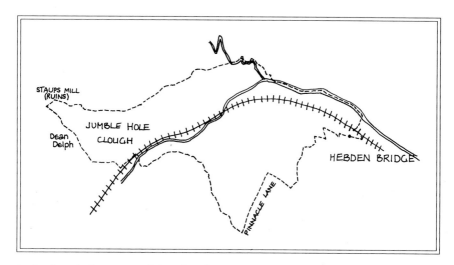

in the clough. As pretty as it is today, this steep-sided little valley was once an important centre of industry, filled with mill-workers and ringing with noise.

At Cow Bridge, cross over the beck and take the path up and around a hair-pin bend. You continue to follow the path of the river, but at a higher level. Pass an old mill-pond and keep climbing, pausing to look at a couple of little waterfalls. When the track bears left, your route is straight ahead, over a stile

These green lanes provide easy walking between fields; the village in the background is Heptonstall

This page: Staup's Mill is now an isolated — and unsafe — ruin in the narrow, wooded confines of Jumble Hole Clough

Opposite: Sturdy stone walls are an ever-present feature of the South Pennine landscape

waymarked "LP", which indicates that this is also a link-path to join the Calderdale Way.

The path is narrower now, and grassy, but it still climbs steadily. Pass through a couple more stiles. The path soon takes you steeply above the clough; there's quite a drop to your right, so watch your step. As you negotiate a further stile you will catch sight of Staup's Mill — now a "romantic" ruin, with just two walls left standing in wooded isolation. Admire the remains of this diminutive old cotton spinning mill — but from a distance, as the unsupported walls are unsafe.

Just above the mill is a waterslide down which the water slithers rather than runs. Cross a footbridge over the beck and climb up stone steps away from the clough and across a narrow field. Turn right at a wall, to follow a paved causeway. Keep to the right of Blackshaw Royd Farm, and follow an indistinct path through fields (take your bearings from stiles in the walls) to keep parallel with Jumble Hole Clough to your right.

When you meet an unmade track, go left for a few yards and then almost immediately right along a track between walls. Pass farm buildings; the Pennine Way crosses your route here, but you just keep left along the main lane to take advantage of breezy, level walking, with splendid views of Stoodley Pike to the right.

Pass a couple more farms, and go through a gate, to walk along a lovely grassy enclosed track. Make your way through a knot of farmhouses, all of which have undergone cosmetic "facelifts". Now you get splendid views down into the valley and your destination of Hebden Bridge, with Heptonstall appearing on the hill opposite at much the same height as you.

Follow a farm track downhill to a tarmac road that's both narrow and steep. Follow it to the right; it descends precipitously into the valley bottom. Look out for a set of steps which cuts the corner off a hairpin bend. You soon arrive back in Hebden Bridge along the Rochdale road. ❑

8. Hardcastle Crags

A 7-mile (13km) walk through one of Calderdale's best-loved beauty spots, and along the top of the Colden valley

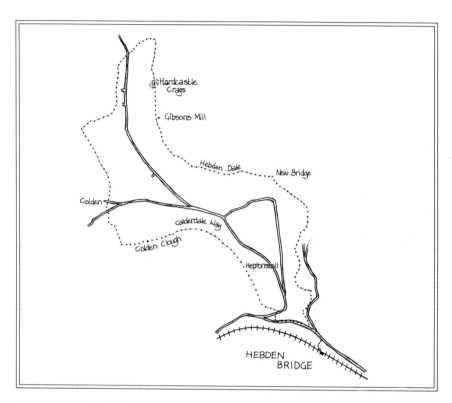

FROM Hebden Bridge station, go up Commercial Street, and cross over St George's Bridge. Go right along Valley Road, and then Victoria Road; at the end of a row of terraced houses go right and then immediately left, past new houses, to a little arched bridge over Hebden Water.

Just across the bridge is a gap in the wall to the right, waymarked "Riverside Walk to Hardcastle Crags". Take this path; it follows the banks of the river into a lovely stretch of woodland, past a cricket pitch and then a bowling green. Here you cross Hebden Water on a metal footbridge, and keep left to follow the river once again.

The path soon leaves the river and approaches a new bungalow. Follow the waymarked steps that rise up ahead of you, between walls. At the top of the steps, go left through more woodland,

73

as you continue to climb. When the path meets a road, cross over and take another short flight of steps, by a National Trust sign that announces you are now entering Spring Wood.

The path meanders through the woodland, which is carpeted with bracken and grasses, and full of songbirds during spring and summer. There are a few boggy bits, though wooden duckboards carry you over the worst.

Soon you are back on the road again; go right. After a mill and houses on the right, take an unmade track on the left. A few yards past a house, take a path to the right which takes you through a field and over a metal footbridge across Hebden Water. Go right after the bridge to follow the course of the river until you reach a stone bridge. Cross it to reach the National Trust car park (Hardcastle Crags are under the aegis of this splendid organisation) and carry on up past the Lodge along the drive. Take the first path to the left, which descends through woodland to Hebden Water.

This area is commonly known as Hardcastle Crags, even though it is more properly the Hebden Valley. People have long appreciated the many woodland and riverside walks along this lovely valley. Yet three times during the last 40 years there have been attempts to flood this area to form yet another reservoir. Fortunately, sounder counsels prevailed, and the valley remains a very popular destination for local people and visitors alike.

The woods are full of birds. You may see spotted flycatchers hawking for flies before returning to their favourite perch. Listen for the drumming of woodpeckers and the summer cadence of the willow warbler.

By the river you meet a well-made path and follow it along the bank. At a riverside clearing called Hebden Hey is a set of stepping stones: a fine place to

break open the sandwiches. Half a mile further on you will see more steppng stones by a little wooden building. After yet another set of stepping stones you will find youself at Gibson Mill.

Despite the idyllic setting, the reason for siting the mill here was purely commercial: the presence of water to power the cotton spinning machines. Nor would the workers at Gibson Mill have found their surroundings particularly romantic. From a report of 1833 we learn that the 22 employees were accustomed to a 72-hour week. The day's work began at 6am and finished at 7.30pm. It's sobering to realise that the two stoppages during this period were for breakfast and dinner.

Another sobering aspect was the prevalence of child labour, with children as young as ten working full days. Because of their small size, children were able to effect running repairs to machines while they were operating. Naturally enough, accidents were commonplace. Men were employed at some mills to keep overworked children awake, often by use of a strap. The owners of Gibson Mill stressed that no such corporal punishment was metered out there. It was not until 1847 that legislation was passed to limit the working day to a maximum of ten hours for women and children.

Gibson Mill was built about 1800; the looms kept up their cacophony for almost 100 years. The building has been seen in other guises: the thousands of visitors who flocked to Hardcastle Crags in the early years of this century could call at the mill for meals and refreshments. For a while it was a ballroom, then a roller skating rink; now it's an evocative memorial to a bygone age.

Carry on past the mill, joining an unmetalled road which climbs up and away from the river. When the track levels off, you will see the crags them-

The River Hebden, as it flows through Hardcastle Crags, provides many places to enjoy a picnic

The well-wooded valley of Hebden Dale — more commonly known as Hardastle Crags — is a popular destination for walkers

selves, to your left. Despite the fact that they have given their name to the whole valley, Hardcastle Crags are an unimpressive outcrop. They are, however, worth the scramble to the top, if only for the splendid views you will have of the wooded valley and the hillsides beyond.

Rejoin the track. When it forks, take the left-hand track and walk parallel to the river, though at a rather higher level. As the path descends you will see a footbridge over the river. Take a left-hand track to double back to the bridge and cross it. Over the bridge, go slightly right to pick up a path that climbs and soon winds to the left and away from the river.

Bear left at the top of the woodland, keeping a wall to your right. Just before a wooden seat, take a track to the right, up to a stile and straight ahead across a field, keeping to the edge by the wall.

Towards the top of the field, bear left to go through a gap in the fence, then through a farmyard to a road. Over the road is a stile and a path crossing a field towards a barn. Go through a gate to the left of the barn, and then keep right of a farmhouse to carry on more or less parallel to the road.

The path is good level walking until the next farm; from here go right, uphill, on an enclosed stony track. Where the track forks, climb to the right to arrive on open moorland.

Carry on until you reach a ruined farm which looks down the valley towards Hebden Bridge. Walk to the end of the clough, where you cross a little beck. You now join the Pennine Way, as you head off to the right in the direction of a farmhouse — Mount Pleasant — on the horizon. This is a moorland land-scape; you will only have sheep and perhaps the odd Pennine Way walker for company. As you pass Mount Pleasant Farm, you get a good view down into the Colden valley.

Make the descent into the valley, leaving the moors behind, to come between walls that converge to form an enclosed track. Cross a minor road, and carry straight on downhill (this is still the Pennine Way, as you will see from the stencilled waymarking). Pass houses to cross a more major road, and find another track in the same direction.

Go left just before a farm, through a little gate, and turn immediately right. Head towards the wooded beginnings of Colden Clough ahead, and go down an enclosed path, which is partly paved. On reaching the woodland, the path becomes steep, and steps have been provided.

Soon you are at a junction of long-distance routes. You should leave the Pennine Way here, and head left beside a wall along a paved causeway which forms part of the Calderdale Way. (First, however, make a little detour: descend the few yards down to Colden Water, a sparkling beck that is spanned by Hebble Hole Bridge. This ancient clapper-style bridge is formed of massive stone slabs. How, you wonder, were they set in place?)

Follow the causeway; this is pleasant walking, as the clough becomes deeper to your right. In places you can see that the paved slabs have been laid on top of low walls, in order to maintain a level surface along the ridge-side.

When the wall does a slight "dog-leg", take a waymarked stile over it. The causeway then crosses a field. Cross a couple more stiles, as the causeway now hugs the edge of a field. The paved path comes to a sudden halt, though your way ahead is unmistakeable. Slightly to your right is Heptonstall, the "new" church being a particularly prominent landmark. You get more extensive views as the clough deepens.

Walk behind a farm, taking your bearings from Heptonstall church. Your path becomes a paved causeway again. Paths branch off, but you should keep to the more obvious main track, along the very top of the clough. When you meet a tarmac road, join it and walk uphill. After 100 yards take a path to the right (waymarked "Calderdale Way") which meanders through dense woodland.

Once you emerge from the trees you will see the spire of Heptonstall church on your left, and a stunning bird's-eye view of the valley down to the right. Stoodley Pike can be seen on the horizon beyond. You walk along the very edge of the clough, above a rocky escarpment: a most exhilarating route. You leave these windy heights to go left on an enclosed track between a clutch of new houses, which are architectural pastiches of the style seen in Heptonstall's older houses. Go right along a track just past the estate.

Go right again on reaching the Heptonstall Social and Bowling Club, along another enclosed path. Keep left by the wall to come out onto the ridge once more, now with extensive views of Hebden Bridge. The path descends steeply, with an even more vertiginous slope to your right (so watch your step). Carry on through woodland until you reach a tarmac road. From here your route is simple: downhill and back into Hebden Bridge. ❑

9. Along the Towpath

A 9-mile (17km) walk along the Calder valley, following the banks of the Rochdale Canal — the first trans-Pennine waterway

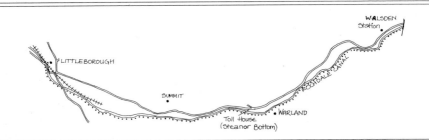

CONSTRUCTION of the Rochdale Canal began in 1799, and was completed five years later. The canal, 32 miles in length from Sowerby Bridge to the centre of Manchester, has 92 locks and more than 100 bridges. It was the first trans-Pennine (the Leeds-Liverpool wasn't finished until 1819), and was for many years a vital link between Lancashire and Yorkshire.

The canal, along with so many others, eventually fell into swift decline, and was abandoned altogether as a navigable waterway during the 1950s. This decline began to be reversed in 1982 when West Yorkshire Metropolitan County Council started a renovation programme which continues to the present.

This trail offers easy level walking all the way from Hebden Bridge to Littleborough. You accompany the Rochdale Canal closely; in only a very few places do you have to leave it at all. If this sounds rather monotonous, be assured that there is much to see at every stage of the walk — some splendid landscapes and relics of the great days of this waterway.

The main road is never far away, and yet the view from the towpath is so very different from the view as seen through a car window. You enter the world of the canal, and begin to understand the rationale behind this way of travelling and transporting goods. You can admire the splendid canal engineering: the locks, bridges, wharfs and warehouses.

Walk from Hebden Bridge station down to the approach road to the canal, and turn left along the towpath, towards town. Pass the marina, and cross over the Black Pit aqueduct. Soon you cross over the canal to join the towpath on the right, and go under Hebble End Bridge.

You come across the ends of terraced houses that back right up to the canal. Beyond a stone bridge is a pub, the Stubbing Wharf. It faces the road, but in summer there are seats put out at the back, along the towpath. As you leave Hebden Bridge you enter woodland.

After you go under a bridge carrying the railway, you will see weirs — cobbled overflow outlets that take excess water away from the canal and down into the river to your right. There are half a dozen of these outfalls encountered between here and Littleborough. To keep your feet dry, you can cross on wooden planks that rest on stone supports. Canal and river here flow side by side, separated only by the width of the towpath.

Just past an old stone bench the canal widens into a broad pool, and cottages

back onto the river and canal. Here — and all along the canal — anglers sit on the bank, surrounded by their rods, nets and other fishing impedimenta. There is certainly no shortage of fish; you may see bream and carp — some quite a size — "grazing" near the surface.

There is a mill on the canal where it widens, and a little arched bridge. The bridge, known as Greenwood's Folly, crosses the river and then comes to a full stop against a mill wall. This spectacularly futile construction is a rather surreal sight.

Past Callis Mill, where the canal renovation project is based, is Callis Bridge. The Pennine Way crosses the canal here; it's the route you take in Walk 7. Just after a sewage farm is a lovely old stone bridge. As you walk underneath it, notice a wooden pole attached to the side of the arch. This was to take the strain of the rope which connected a barge and the horse pulling it. Better for the rope to rub against wood than to become frayed by the stonework. You can see the deep grooves in the pole which the ropes

have cut. Nevertheless, further along the canal you can see similar grooves in the stonework too.

Your surroundings are still well-wooded and tranquil as you pass a cricket pitch and more cottages whose gardens go right down to the canalside. Past Shawplains Lock the woods recede on the left, as the canal winds through open fields. On your right the railway line goes over a viaduct; on the left a jagged rock face indicates the site of an old quarry.

You begin to see houses on the right, announcing that the centre of Todmorden isn't far away. A mill by the left bank of the canal once belonged to Thomas Binns, and wooden clogs were made here. A tall chimney stands alone, a few yards from the mill building.

The valley broadens as you enter Todmorden. Depending on the time of day, and the season of the year, you should be seeing more people hereabouts. It's good to see that the canal and its environs are so well used — and not merely by those who navigate the locks in narrowboats. You'll see lovers and loners, hikers and bikers, sun-seekers, lunch-eaters, joggers and kids.

You pass a modern engineering works on the right, and a landing wharf on the left. In Todmorden you find plenty of mills and warehouses at the canalside, and friendly pubs too, if you arrive during opening hours.

TODMORDEN
Station
ROCHDALE CANAL
HEBDEN BRIDGE

Rows of terraced houses back up to the towpath, as the Rochdale Canal heads from Hebden Bridge towards Todmorden

A little tunnel takes you underneath the main road, and you must now cross the canal too, as the towpath continues from here along the left-hand side. As you round a bend you will see the Great Wall of Todmorden — a huge retaining wall built to stop the hillside and the railway from falling into the canal. The brick-built wall is truly a splendid sight.

As you pass the great wall, look up to the right to see Dobroyd Castle (now a school). Soon the canal goes under the elaborate railway bridge at Gauxholme, complete with castellated towers. There are many locks along this section, as the canal gradually rises. Look out on the right for a fine example of a canalside warehouse. Barges could go right inside, through an archway, to have their cargoes of cotton and coal unloaded. They would be loaded up with finished fabrics for the return journey.

Cross beneath the railway once more, which now runs over a more utilitarian iron bridge. At a new bridge you join the towpath — now a broad gravel track — to the right of the canal. Pass Smithyholme and Pinnel locks, and, as you cross over a bridge, look to the right to see the newly reopened railway station at Walsden; this provides a quick way back to Hebden Bridge if you wish to walk no further.

Here are mills that come to the very edge of the canal, and trees whose branches bend over the water. This must have been a bustling scene when the canal was paying its way, instead of being the recreational amenity that is has become. As the canal runs parallel with the road, a row of terraced houses backs onto the towpath, including the Cross Keys pub.

After the Nip Square Lock the canal

People — and wildlife — are flocking back to the Rochdale Canal, now that it is navigable once again; this is Todmorden

broadens into another pool. The landscape changes too, from the mills and terraces of Todmorden into a scene that's typically Pennine: steep slopes, wooded cloughs, dry-stone walls and hill farms.

Bird i' th' Hand, an old coaching Inn, built to capitalise on the traffic along the turnpiked road. In between Warland Upper Lock and a swing-bridge is a modern boundary stone, which an-

The Rochdale Canal widens here, between Hebden Bridge and Todmorden, to provide a good spot for local fishermen

This section arguably provides the best walking of the day.

The canal supports a good deal of wildlife. The banks have a proliferation of rushes, grasses and flowers, among which little electric-blue dragonflies hover. Moorhens, modest little birds, swim in and out of the banksides. There are multi-coloured ducks of indeterminate species; they are Mallard hybrids. Mute Swans swim regally along the canal, and wagtails search for food along the margins.

At Lock 34 look to the right to see the

nounces that you are crossing over from Yorkshire into Lancashire.

A white house — at one time a lockkeeper's cottage — sits beside Longlees Lock. If you look to the right you will see a curious little six-sided building on what was once the junction of turnpike roads. This is Steanor Bottom Toll House, built in 1824, and a field path leads directly to it if you want to take a closer look at this fascinating relic of transport history. On the front of the building, above the door, is a replica of the tariff board which features the toll charges for the various

A lock-keeper's cottage sits beside Longlees Lock on the Rochdale Canal, just south of Walsden

categories of traffic. These charges were levied until 1878.

Back at the canal, keep walking through this splendid landscape. Look out for a little arch in the opposite bank of the canal; this is an overflow from nearby Lower Chelburn Reservoir.

After the Summit Locks, it's downhill all the way to Littleborough. Not that you are likely to notice the difference, so gentle is the gradient. On your left you will see another old quarry, and on the right the cluster of houses that comprises Summit. You pass along the back of an old mill before arriving at Courtaulds, a mill that's still very much in business.

If you have been wondering where the trains have gone, the answer is simple. They've disappeared into the hillside, via the Summit tunnel. If you look right here you will see the line reappearing through the tunnel entrance.

There is more splendid countryside as you approach Littleborough. Enjoy, too, the new and refurbished lock gates: signs of the amount of hard work expended on re-establishing this stretch of the canal as a navigable waterway. Soon you will see a little side channel of the canal just long enough to accommodate a barge.

You are in Littleborough almost before you know it; watch out for the railway station on your right, only a few yards from the canal towpath. As you take the train back to Hebden Bridge you can enjoy seeing what will now be familiar landmarks from a comfortable seat. ❏

10. Historic Heptonstall

This splendid weavers' village escaped the industrialisation that changed the valley below so dramatically

THE hill village of Heptonstall is one of the highlights of any tour of the South Pennines. In its heyday the village thrived on a dual economy of hill-farming and hand-weaving; some fine stone houses testify to its success. This prosperity was won at a time when Hebden Bridge, in the valley beneath, was the lesser settlement.

With the coming of the Industrial Revolution, however, the fortunes of Heptonstall and Hebden Bridge were reversed. The rivers Hebden and Calder provided the motive power for the mills being built in the valley bottom. For Heptonstall, perched on a hillside without access to such water power, industrial opportunities were denied. It was left, quite literally, high and dry.

Thus it was that Heptonstall remained largely untouched by the dramatic changes that were seen elsewhere in the South Pennines. Here is preserved, almost untouched, a pre-industrial village. The clusters of weavers' cottages huddle together against the elements; it almost seems they have repelled the ravages of time.

Heptonstall has no need of any "heritage centre"; the old village is handsomely authentic, and unspoiled by tea-rooms and gift-shops. The many interesting features can be seen at a canter in less than an hour, but if you have time to spare you can slow down and soak up the atmosphere. You can hardly help yourself going back in time.

From Hebden Bridge station, walk into the centre of town. Cross the old packhorse bridge, and take the steep cobbled path to the left, known as Buttress. Turn right at the top, and walk along the road for a few yards, before picking up a set of steep steps on the left. This is a direct way up to Heptonstall. Car drivers should park in Heptonstall car park, reached by a narrow alleyway; the walk begins here.

At the top of the car park is a wall with four windows — all different — and a little wooden door at the bottom. The building was once the brew-house to a long-vanished pub, the Stag, and the little door led into a windowless lock-up where offenders could be held temporarily until they could be taken to a proper prison.

Nearer the car park entrance is an old well and a passageway on the right that takes you up steps, past Stag Cottage — one of the oldest dwellings in Heptonstall — and out onto the cobbles of Towngate.

Turn almost immediately right, into Northgate. The first house on the right is called Litherstone; Methodist meetings were held in a room here between 1748 and 1764, before a chapel was built.

On the opposite side of Northgate is New House. Look up to find a delightful carved stone panel over the door. The panel features a date — 1736 — and a trio of initials — H E F — which refer to Henry and Elizabeth Foster. Such date-stones are common in the area, but this one is unusual in also featuring little carved representations of the couple themselves.

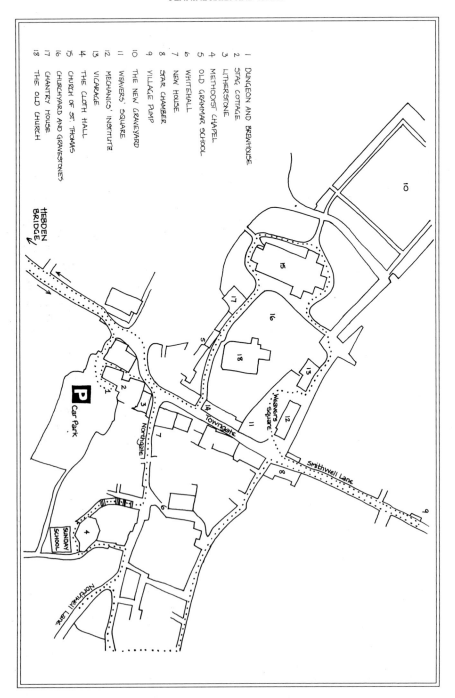

1 DUNGEON AND BREWHOUSE
2 STAG COTTAGE
3 LITHERSTONE
4 METHODIST CHAPEL
5 OLD GRAMMAR SCHOOL
6 WHITEHALL
7 NEW HOUSE
8 STAR CHAMBER
9 VILLAGE PUMP
10 THE NEW GRAVEYARD
11 WEAVERS' SQUARE
12 MECHANICS' INSTITUTE
13 VICARAGE
14 THE CLOTH HALL
15 CHURCH OF ST. THOMAS
16 CHURCHYARD AND GRAVESTONES
17 CHANTRY HOUSE
18 THE OLD CHURCH

HEBDEN BRIDGE

Car Park

Weavers Square

Smithwell Lane

Towngate

Northgate

SUNDAY SCHOOL

Northwell Lane

Many Calderdale houses bear datestones over the front door, but this example in Heptonstall features these delightful portraits too

A few yards further on is another date-stone — this time on an archway spanning a narrow lane. The carved initials (I B) are those of John Bentley, and the house seen on the left through the arch was for many years in the hands of the Bentley family.

Soon you take steps to the right down to the Methodist Chapel, a splendid octagonal building that has the distinction of being the oldest Methodist chapel in continuous use for its original purpose. Methodism first came to the area in 1742, and the Rev John Wesley himself came to preach in the village on a number of occasions.

The chapel was built to Wesley's own specifications, the octagonal shape being chosen to emphasise that it was a preaching chapel and not a church. According to Wesley, this shape also offered "no corner in which the devil can hide". The chapel was completed in 1764. Thirty years later a Sunday School was inaugurated; the building is adjacent to the chapel.

The society thrived — so much so that the symmetrical chapel had to be enlarged. One end was dismantled, and two walls were extended; this maintained the octagonal shape.

The rather severe external appearance belies what you find inside (it is usually open during the day). Seating is on the double-decker principle, with an extensive gallery. The walls, ceiling and other details are picked out in pastel blue and pink. There is an orderly array of boxed pews on both levels, and sumptuous red carpeting on the floor. The overall effect is very tranquil.

Walk between the chapel and the

The lovely old Methodist chapel at Heptonstall was built to an octagonal design approved by John Wesley himself

Sunday School; through an archway take the little path — Tinker Bank — which leads back up to Northgate. Go right to investigate the start of Northwell Lane, which was once part of an old packhorse route between Heptonstall and Haworth. The Calderdale Way follows this track, as far as Pecket Well.

Carry on along Northgate, going left and left again to bring you past a row of pebble-dashed prefabricated houses (quite a shock after the architectural unity of the other buildings in the village) and onto Towngate again.

Turn right up the hill. Today Heptonstall has two pubs, the White Lion and the Cross Inn. In the village's heyday, however, there were a grand total of seven inns — to cater for the various needs of locals, traders and travellers. If seven inns seems an excessive number, it should be remembered that Heptonstall was once a busy centre in the weaving industry.

A house a little further up Towngate is called Star Chamber, though the reason for this name is speculative. The Star Chamber was the infamous London court which, until it was disbanded in 1641, was known for the severity of its sentences. A trial in the 16th century — at about the time the house was built — had involved some Heptonstall people.

On either side of the street are sturdy terraced houses; this area is called Top O'the Town. Pass Silver Street on the left, to reach the old village pump, set within an arched recess and bearing the date 1891.

Stroll back down Towngate and turn right into Weaver's Square, an open area formed when some old weavers' cottages were demolished in 1968. Walk into Church Street, noticing the Mechanics' Institute on the right. A plaque on the wall is dated 1868 and bears the instructive legend "Man know thyself". Walk past the Vicarage, as the cobbled lane becomes stony. (Ahead of you is the new graveyard, where the poet Sylvia Plath is buried.)

Turn left into the churchyard. This is one of the most evocative churchyards you could ever hope to see — not least because it is shared, almost uniquely, by two churches. Take a look first at the new church to the right. The interior is remarkably spacious, considering the size of the village itself, and the fixtures and fittings were updated, not without some controversy, in the 1960s. You can make your own judgement about the aesthetics of the modern furnishings, and compare them with the old layout — as seen on photographs in the church.

A homely touch is provided, however, by the kneeling hassocks, which are hand-woven and feature all manner of religious icons: white doves, crosses, crowns, biblical quotations, and even that famous ecclesiastical figure, Micky Mouse!

Another surprise is to find a copy of Leonardo da Vinci's painting of The Last Supper hanging on the north wall. This was painted in 1905 for the government of Italy, because the original fresco painting was found to be in an unstable condition. The copy was bought, however, by a Hebden Bridge man, and was subsequently donated to the church.

The old chapel is now a picturesque ruin, though John Wesley was moved to call it, when he preached here in 1876, "the ugliest church I know". The chapel was built in the 13th century, though most of the remains you can see today date from the 15th century, when the building was increased in size to accommodate a growing congregation. The church was dedicated to Thomas à Becket, who was canonised shortly after his murder in Canterbury Cathedral.

In 1847 a storm damaged much of the tower, and plans were made to erect a new church, to be financed by public

The old Heptonstall church, dedicated to Thomas à Becket, is now merely a picturesque ruin

The churchyard at Heptonstall, paved with gravestones, is almost unique in being shared by two churches

subscription. However, services were still being held in the old chapel up to 1854, when the new church, dedicated to St Thomas the Apostle, was finished. Fixtures were removed from the old chapel, which soon deteriorated into a ruinous state.

It is said that thousands of people have been buried in the graveyard. Certainly, the stone slabs which now lie side by side have many names inscribed on them. Some of the slabs are known to be inscribed on the underside too. The earliest dated gravestone bears the year of 1501.

Of all the graves, two are worthy of note. David Hartley, leader of the Crag Vale Coiners, was hanged in 1770 at York, for his part in the illegal clipping of gold coins. The clippings were melted down and recast, to produce counterfeit coins.

David Hartley lived at Bell House, in Crag Vale, which is visited during walk number 13. To find his gravestone, walk about ten yards from the south porch of the old chapel in the direction of the new church. There is, however, no mention on the stone of either his crimes or his subsequent punishment.

More informative — though no less salutary — is a gravestone to be found just to the left of the north porch of the new church. It reads as follows: "In memory of William Greenwood of Pecket Well, who was found dead at Bridgewellhead, in Wadsworth, on the 14th day of August, 1820. He was forsaken by a bad wife, who forced him to serve his majesty in the 3rd York Militia for 8 years. He left a girl aged 16 years, to be cozen'd by her mother's father, out of his money. His own father deposed for felony, his own ·brother, James Greenwood, who was arraigned before a magistrate, for his raiment which he had bequeathed to him before his death in the presence of two witnesses. His thread of life now spun, his age near thirty five years, and in his trouble dropped down and left this vale of tears.

Having investigated this remarkable mosaic of old gravestones, notice the Chantry House which fronts directly onto the graveyard. This was once the charnel house, where human bones were kept. When the buildings were converted into cottages, the entrance doors had to be moved. This is because only church properties could have direct access to churchyards.

A few yards away is the old grammer school, founded in 1642 by the Rev Charles Greenwood, the Lord of the Manor of Heptonstall. The school bell was rung for the last time in 1898, when the premises were acquired by the Yorkshire Penny Bank. Fortunately, much of the school interior was retained; its most recent incarnation was as a museum, but is now sadly closed to the public.

As you rejoin Towngate, through an archway, you will see the Old Cloth Hall on your left. Opened for business in 1545, this is where the hand-loom weavers of Heptonstall would offer their woven fabrics for sale to dealers. For almost 100 years this was the only cloth hall in the whole of the South Pennines. From here you turn right to re-enter the car park, or make your way back down into Hebden Bridge. ❑

11. Hebden Bridge Town Trail

A wander round a fascinating town whose fortunes were won from the textile industries, and is now reborn as a destination for visitors

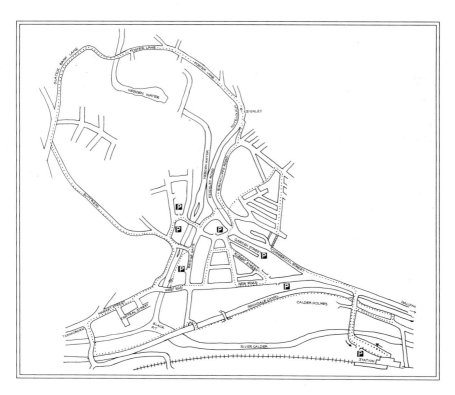

LEAVE Hebden Bridge station through the car park; walk down the road and cross over the River Calder. As you approach the canal, turn right down a short road to arrive at the towpath. Turn left and accompany the canal; once under the bridge you will see that the buildings on the opposite side back directly onto the water. On your left is a park and a children's playground.

Soon, on the right, you will see the marina: a canal basin and open space where people can sit, relax and watch the comings and goings of the barges. The marina is a recent amenity, and uses part of the original canal wharf which had previously been filled in.

Calder Valley Cruising runs a narrowboat service along the canal. The barges are often horse-drawn, particularly at weekends, and you can book both the *Sarah Siddons* and the *Gracie Fields* for private parties and other functions. Telephone (0422) 844833 for further information.

beyond the shop-fronts to appreciate them.

For those who tire of chain stores and seemingly identical shopping malls, Hebden Bridge offers a wonderful vari-

Thanks to extensive renovations, the railway station at Hebden Bridge looks much as it did at the turn of the century

Carry on walking along the towpath, under a concrete footbridge. Cross the canal at a fine old stone bridge, adjacent to Blackpit Lock. Follow the towpath along the other side. If you look down to your right you will see that the canal crosses Black Pit (the confluence of the rivers Calder and Hebden) on an aqueduct, which remains the largest structure on the Rochdale Canal.

Walk along the towpath for about 100 yards, leaving the canal by going right at Hebble End Bridge. Cross the river again and turn right into Market Street. It is lined with shops, many of which have elaborate façades and windows — even though you have to raise your eyes

ety of speciality shops, along Market Street and elsewhere. The hippy influx of a few years back leaves the town with a rich legacy of hand-thrown pottery, "stained glass" ornaments, mobiles, and other indispensible items of frippery.

A handsome building set back from the road was originally built as Ebenezer Chapel, in 1777, which accounts for the presence of gravestones on the lawn at the front. In more recent times it has

Right: "Top and bottom" houses at Hebden Bridge provided accommodation for millworkers' families on two levels

St George's Bridge and Bridge Mill, sited here in order to use the motive power of the water in the River Hebden

served as an arts centre, and is now an antiques shop.

Just before the road crosses the river on West End Bridge, bear left along Old Gate and accompany the river for a short way. You soon reach the old packhorse bridge (more about this later) and then, on your left, Buttress — a paved path providing an uncompromisingly steep climb for pedestrians up to Heptonstall village. This is a very old pathway; it remains "unimproved" simply because it is too steep to be upgraded into a road

suitable for vehicular use. (The next stretch of the walk involves some strenuous climbing; if you want a more abbreviated stroll, just take a short cut to St George's Bridge, a few yards away).

Walk up Buttress; the climb is steep, but at least there's a hand-rail. From the top of the path you will be rewarded by splendid panoramic views of Hebden Bridge, its rows of tall terraced houses sticking limpet-like to the steep contours of the valley sides.

When you reach a road at the top of

the cobbled path, turn right for a few yards, then turn right almost immediately down an unmade road. This is Slater Bank and leads straight down to the driveway of a house. At this point you turn half right to take a steep cobbled path which descends between walls. Ignore tracks bearing off to the right, and then left, to arrive at the River Hebden. Just before a bridge is a sign, pointing left, which indicates a riverside walk to Hardcastle Crags. Walk 8 takes this delightful riverside path up to the justly famous beauty spot.

Cross the river on an old stone bridge, pass a group of new houses and walk up Foster Lane until you meet the main Keighley road by the Nutclough House Hotel. Nutclough Mill was the site of one of the first manufacturing co-opera-tives, the Hebden Bridge Fustian Manufacturing Society. (Fustian was a type of cloth that was cut to give a thick "pile").

Cross the road and bear right up to Eiffell Buildings, a row of four-storey terraced houses; the road soon becomes Birchcliffe Street. Near the bottom, take steps to the right, then a cobbled path, and cross Keighley road once again.

Go right into Bridge Gate; the first building on the right is the White Lion. It was built in 1657, as a farm rather than an inn, though most of the façade has since been renovated. The pub used to provide a welcome halt for travellers on trans-Pennine stagecoach journeys.

St George's Square, ahead, provides an open space in the middle of town. From here, cross the river on the iron St George's Bridge. The adjacent Bridge

The packhorse bridge at Hebden Bridge, at the meeting of a number of ancient tracks, is still much used today by pedestrians

Mill stands on a site once occupied by a mill where corn was ground, though the building that can be seen today is about 200 years old. The mill chimney was put up about 1820, when steam power was introduced.

Once across the bridge, you see the council offices on your left, with their splendid late-Victorian façade. Turn left, seeing Buttress rising steeply to the right, and the Hole in the Wall pub.

Ahead of you is the old packhorse bridge — a fine three-arched edifice and the origin of the town's name, as it spans the River Hebden just a few yards before it joins the Calder at Black Pit. Early records indicate that the present structure (replacing an earlier wooden bridge) was built about 1510, and was paid for by legacies from prominent local people.

The bridge was at a junction of important packhorse routes (Buttress is the start of one track), so there was every incentive to build inns, blacksmiths' forges and other businesses to capitalise on the influx of travellers. The bridge has been consolidated on a number of occasions, with each repair (1602, 1657, 1845 and 1890) proudly recorded on plaques set into the side of the bridge.

Triangular recesses in the bridge provided sanctuary for people who found themselves on the bridge at the same time as laden ponies were crossing. This was necessary because the ponies' panniers would take up the full 7ft 6ins width of the bridge.

The bridge, and the little area just south of it, was renovated yet again in 1977; it's quite a magnet for people with time on their hands, to come and sit, feed the ducks, eat their lunchtime sandwiches or just watch the world go by. The bridge seems to be as much the centre of town as it ever was.

Follow a little path along the river; it joins the main road just by the Tourist Information Centre, which is stocked with a bewildering array of information about the area.

Turn left at the main road, and walk past the traffic lights. As you go left again, up Crown Street, look at the National Westminster Bank — built in 1870 but in a style that belongs to two centuries earlier. At the top of Crown Street is a splendid building with a clock tower, which occupies a corner site. It was once the premises of the Hebden Bridge Co-operative Society, and is now a hotel. A fire escape spans Carlton Street at first-floor level. Turn right along Carlton Street and right again: Hope Street. Go left at New Road.

This is your chance to investigate more closely the canal basin that you saw earlier from the opposite side of the water. Recross the main road and head up Albert Street. Oxford House, on the right, boasts an elaborate façade, with balconies at the upstairs windows. Like so many of the buildings in Hebden Bridge, Oxford House has been sandblasted to reveal the pristine stone beneath the accumulated layers of industrial grime.

At the top of Albert Street, go right to meet the Keighley road. Here is the old Hollins Toll Bar House, where dues were collected from travellers coming from the direction of Halifax along the turnpike road.

Cross the road and head up Birch Place. To the left of Stubbings School — opened in 1878 — is a narrow cobbled path which takes you up the hill, at the backs of houses. This is another of the packhorse routes which radiated out from the old bridge. Pause for breath at the top, then go right uphill, along Birchcliffe Road. From here you will get extensive views over Hebden Bridge, in its superb valley setting. There are seats put thoughtfully here, if you want to rest your legs and enjoy the scene.

Go right down Marlborough Street to

join Osborne Street. This area, comprising tall terraced houses, is the Stubbings Improvement Area. These houses represent an unusual response, during the last century, to the equally unusual terrain of Hebden Bridge. On these dramatically steep sites, the terraced houses present a four-storey appearance from the valley, but show just two storeys when seen from above.

They were erected when space in the expanding town was at a premiun, and enabled two families to live "up" and "down", while giving them both access at street level: a neat solution to a knotty architectural problem. A programme of improvement grants has, in recent years, given these characterful dwellings a new lease of life.

On Osborne Street you will see the Zion Baptist Chapel where, in an area well-known for nonconformist religions, a strict form of the Baptist faith is adhered to. A few yards up the road is a long flight of 106 steps which descends vertiginously into Commercial Street far below.

At the bottom of the steps, go left along Commercial Street, and take a look at a trio of interesting houses. Southcliffe House has a courtyard and stables at the back, and a mounting block at the side to help horse-riders onto their mounts. Nearby Machpelah House is a handsome town house that was once the home of Dr John Fawcett, a well-known Baptist minister. The next building is a three-storey workshop for the cutting of fustian. Note the end wall of the top floor, with its grand total of 29 narrow mullioned windows to throw as much light as possible onto the cutters' work.

You have just joined the main Halifax road; the entrance to the railway station is no more than a minute's walk to the left. ❑

The canal basin has been renovated in recent years; from here you can travel through the locks on a traditional narrow-boat

12. Limers Gate and Luddenden Dean

An 11-mile (19km) walk from Hebden Bridge to Sowerby Bridge, which uses an ancient pack-horse way over high moorland

AS you begin this walk from Hebden Bridge station, make sure you have a large-scale map of the area. From the station, follow the station drive to the park gates on the left. Walk along the right-hand edge of the park and cross the first bridge over the canal. Continue straight across the small park to the road by the traffic lights. Cross over by the Tourist Information Centre and walk down Bridge Gate to the hump-backed bridge across Hebden Water that gives the town its name.

Cross the bridge and turn right down Hangingroyd Lane. At the road junction turn right and then left over the bridge. Walk along the street of terraced houses down to another old bridge, passing the base of an old mill chimney on the way. Go over the bridge and turn immediately right, along a waymarked path that accompanies the river Hebden. (If you have already done Walk 8, then this riverside section will be familiar).

Walk up the valley, past a bowling green, to reach a footbridge. Cross over the bridge and continue along the riverside path to a road.

Take the stone steps opposite which lead into an area of attractive deciduous woodland owned by the National Trust. Follow the path parallel to the road which it later rejoins. Walk along the road until the next left turning down a track. Follow the track past a house, then turn right onto a field path that leads to a footbridge. Follow the signed Calderdale Way footpath to New Bridge. Re-cross the river and continue past the Lodge to the car park in Hardcastle Crags.

At the car park take the steps on the right of the information board and continue straight ahead to join a stony track up into Crimsworth Dean. Pass through the mainly coniferous woodland to emerge finally onto open moorland. Continue along the track, past a farm house with views of Cock Hill on the other side of the valley. Take the green track bearing right, signposted Lumb Bridge, down to the valley bottom.

Lumb Bridge itself is exquisitely set in a shady glade, framed by waterfalls. This was one of the many bridges built along Limers Gate packhorse route. There are two such routes in the area which are known as Limers Gate; one goes from Rochdale to Clitheroe while this one links Boulsworth Hill near Wycoller, to Luddenden and the farms around Halifax.

The name Limers refers to lime, huge quantities of which were transported by pack-ponies in the 17th and 18th centuries from limestone areas in Craven and Bowland to neutralise the acidic Pennine soils. "Gate" is a Yorkshire dialect word, derived from Old Norse, and simply means a road.

Cross over Lumb Bridge and skirt the edge of the falls, before climbing up an enclosed way — still paved in places — to a lane. Turn right, walking past Gib

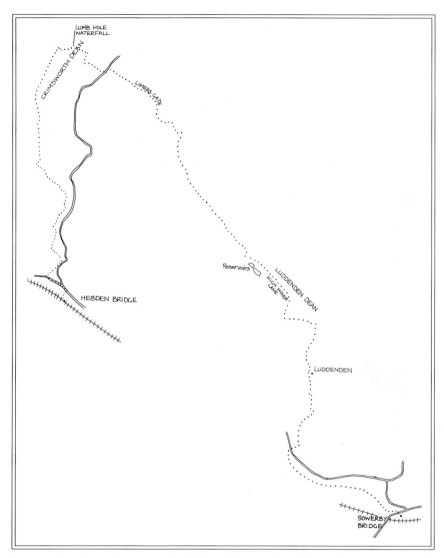

Farm and go through a gate on the left to join an enclosed track. Go through a second gate and swing slightly to the right; then continue along a rough track up to the road that links Keighley and Hebden Bridge.

Cross the road and walk a few yards up the hill to the wall end. Turn right, walking up a rather marshy slope fol-lowing the wall. As the slope flattens out it should be possible to pick up the faint path that leads to a stony outcrop above, almost directly in line with the wall you have been following.

At the rocks, look towards a cairn about 100 yards ahead. Make for it to join a path marked by a line of cairns to the triangulation point. This is along the

Crimsworth Dean provides lovely woodland walking before climbing to follow Limers Gate, an old packhorse way

line of the old packhorse route; at one time, trains of 20 to 30 ponies would come this way, led by the packman or jagger.

The name "jagger" is derived from the German *jaeger*, meaning hunting ponies: short stocky animals once popular for this work. Each animal would have carried 2-3 cwts (1 cwt equals about 50 kilos); long before you saw them you would have heard the faint tinkle of bells from the lead animal, the "Bell Horse", warning of their approach.

As you approach the white trig point on the summit of the moor, you can see Wharley Moor reservoir in the distance. On a clear day you should be able to stand at the trig point and look right across Yorkshire to Holme Moss, Pendle Hill and Pen-y-Ghent.

Turn left for a few yards before picking up a faint path leading down to a blue marker post. Continue straight ahead until you reach a concrete drainage channel; turn left following it to a stone bridge. (If by any chance the drainage channel is missed, in bad weather, continue to Castle Carr boundary wall and follow it round to cross Black Clough).

Turn right and follow a ditch, and take the left fork following the blue marker posts down to the Castle Carr boundary wall. Cross the stream at Black

Clough and follow the wall contouring along the valley side. From here you can see the ruins of the 19th century house and its two castellated gate-houses amidst the trees.

Continue straight ahead following the line of old wooden fence posts, past the renovated barn onto a metalled track. On your left is Luddenden Dean, one of Calderdale's most beautiful valleys. Past two houses take the right fork; here the road becomes a sandy track which gradually descends to join a road. Continue straight ahead, ignoring the two lanes leading down to the valley bottom. Keep going past some farms and look for an old horse trough built into the wall on your right. Opposite is a footpath sign leading down to a track.

Cross the track and continue through the farm. Notice the handsome Victorian barn on your left, complete with dove-cote. Walk in front of houses, go down the stone steps in the corner and follow the footpath down to a track. Turn right, following Luddenden Brook which used to power the wheels of early mills.

The track joins a cobbled lane. On the other side of the river is the cemetery; the lane finally leads into the churchyard of St Mary the Virgin. William Grimshaw, the famous 18th century hell-fire preacher from Haworth, is buried here.

Luddenden is a village of sharp corners, narrow streets and small stone dwellings. If time permits, call in at the Lord Nelson Inn. It dates from 1634, as can be seen from the datestone over the door. Originally called the White Swan, it was renamed to commemorate Nelson's victory at Trafalgar.

The pub is best known as one of the haunts of Branwell Brontë, who was employed as a ticket clerk at Luddenden Foot station. He worked there for only a

A break in the clouds lights up a group of houses in the valley of Luddenden Dean

The ancient weavers' village of Heptonstall stands on its hill-top site, with the monument of Stoodley Pike in the distance

few months, being dismissed because of discrepancies in the accounts.

Turn left down the street, over the bridge and then turn right down a cobbled lane along the river. At the road, continue straight ahead past a road junction. Walk on for a short distance, looking for a footpath sign on the left. The footpath runs between two houses, down some steps and then over a bridge. Turn left and then sharp right at the rocky outcrop to a gap-stile.

Bear right, cutting diagonally across the field. Go through the gateway and continue to the left-hand corner of the field. Through the stile, keep the farmhouse on your right, and walk up the field to join a lane. Walk along the lane; ignore the road swinging to the right down to Luddenden Foot and continue past Magson House Farm. As you approach the edge of the housing estate, look for a footpath on the right. Go down the steep steps into the valley and join the main road.

Cross the road and turn right for a few yards; then turn left down a cobbled lane over the canal bridge and onto the towpath. Turn right and follow the canal into Sowerby Bridge. This is a particularly peaceful section of the canal. As you approach Sowerby Bridge, look out for the double-decker houses on the side of the canal — literally two houses built on top of one another, utilising the steep sides of the Calder Valley.

The Rochdale Canal, filled in after the Second World War, now ends in a car park. Continue across the car park and turn right at the public conveniences. Cross the road, take a ginnel almost opposite and go over a bridge. Turn left to arrive at Sowerby Bridge railway station. ❑

13. Cragg Vale and the Coiners

A 6-mile (11km) walk from Hebden Bridge to Mytholmroyd, through a notorious haunt of counterfeiters

FROM Hebden Bridge station entrance, turn right down a tarmac track, and go under the railway bridge. Continue straight ahead past the new houses on your right, and then take the walled track on your right up the hill. Ignore the first left-hand turn, but continue straight ahead, to a second turning signed "Mytholmroyd and Old Chamber". From here there are magnificent views of Hebden Bridge.

This is an old pathway through the woods and you can still see the remains of flagstones. At the stile follow the field path towards Old Chamber, once a small thriving hamlet of five farmsteads. At the wooden stile swing right to the yellow waymarker to the right of the sheep pens to a stile, almost hidden by trees, and onto a track.

Take the path opposite and cut diagonally across the field to a stile, to the right of two gates. Follow the wall to a track and go past a house; your route gradually becomes a green track contouring around the hillside. Just before the clump of birch trees, look for two old gate posts marking a sunken track on your right.

Follow the track up the hillside. In some places it is rather overgrown and you may need to walk to the right of it. Continue to a wire fence and a stile leading onto open moorland. Cross the stile and, while still ascending, bear left up to the far wall corner. Straight ahead you can see Stoodley Pike and an old stone waymarker, which once defined the boundary of the Erringden Deer Park.

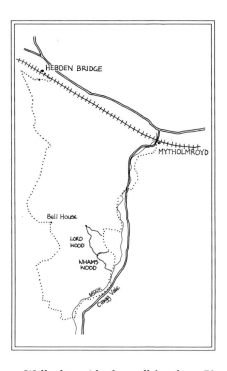

Walk alongside the wall for about 50 yards and then turn right to follow the line of a collapsed wall towards the valley head. Down below is Erringden Wood. This was once part of the Erringden Deer Park constructed by the de Warrens, Earls of Surrey during the 12th and 13th centuries. The park originally covered 3,000 acres extending over the moorland. Higher up the moors you can still see the deer leap, a deep trench built to prevent the deer escaping.

At the valley head continue round the edge of the valley towards Bell House.

The path gradually becomes clearer and is paved in places. Bell House was at one time the home of David Hartley, the notorious Cragg Vale coiner.

During the 18th century, the clipping and counterfeiting of gold coins was rife, and became a matter of national cause, although they were legal tender, they were not as well known as the English Guinea.

Naturally, the coiners' activities were soon discovered. William Deighton was appointed as the excise officer in charge of suppressing the gang. He arrested

Bell House was the home of David Hartley, who was hanged in 1770 for his part in the counterfeiting of coins

concern. One of the main centres of this illicit activity was around Mytholmroyd and Cragg Vale, and it was estimated that 3,500 "Real Portuguese" coins were counterfeited hereabouts. "King David" clipped gold from the edges of the coins, and then produced more coins by melting down these clippings.

Stamping the designs on the coins required considerable skill. Just the right amount of pressure had to be applied to the die, to ensure the design was clearly embossed without splitting the coin. The coiners chose Portuguese Moidore be-

several prominent coiners, including David Hartley, who were taken to York Castle. In response, a group of coiners, led by Isaac Hartley, David's brother, murdered Deighton in Halifax.

David Hartley was hanged in York in 1770 for his part in these crimes; he is now buried in Heptonstall churchyard. Isaac Hartley escaped prosecution, but many of the other coiners were arrested after Deighton's murder. However, it was some time before coin clipping was finally outlawed.

At Bell House turn right across the

moorland to join a rough track. After a few yards turn right again and continue to bear slightly right. Make for a wall corner, and bend right up the slope across the moorland. As you climb, you should see the chimney pots of Stony Royd Farm in the distance. Head for this farm-house, following the wall to a stone stile.

Cross the stile and walk past the farm-house. Look for a metal gate on the right before you reach the track. Go through the gate and make for the stile on the right-hand side of the field. Cross the stile and go through a gate be-fore crossing an-other field and down to a second gate onto a track. From here there is a superb view of Withens Clough Reservoir with Stoodley Pike monument be-hind.

On reaching the track, go through the first gate on the right. Descend towards a step-stile at the top of the wood below. Continue walking down the hillside, keeping to the wall. At the bottom corner there is a stone step-stile down to the track which is rather hidden and is actu-ally best seen from the other side.

Turn left down the track past Swan Bank Farm, forking left to zig-zag down the hill. Look out for Old Cragg Hall, built in the 17th century but with a fine early-19th century porch displaying the

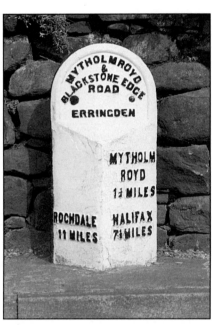

A sign that recalls the days of the Blackstone Edge turnpike

arms of Christopher Rawson.

Continue down the road, turning left into the small hamlet of Cragg, with its early Victorian church and a pub, the Hinchcliffe Arms, named after the Hin-cliffe family which owned several of the mills in Cragg Vale. They achieved no-toriety during the 1830s, when the ap-palling conditions in one of their mills were revealed in a report by George Crabtree, who was then fighting for a working day of no more than ten hours, and restrictions on child labour.

Cragg Vale and Mytholmroyd emerged as real black spots. It was said that some chil-dren worked in the Hinchcliffe mills from 5.30 in the morning until 8.30 at night, and were fre-quently fined — or beaten — if they were late. Crabtree quoted the Rev Sherman Crowther, vicar of St John's church in Cragg: "The Cragg Vale mill-owners are a pest and disgrace to society; laws human and divine are insuf-fient to restrain them".

If you walk around the graveyard at Cragg, you will find headstones that reveal a disturbing number of ex-fac-tory children who died under the age of twelve.

Go left over the bridge, down a sign-posted lane, through a narrow green gate. Walk along the riverside path to an old bridge. At the bridge continue

The wooded valley of Cragg Vale is associated with the Coiners, a gang of counterfeiters who illicitly clipped the edges of coins

straight ahead along a track for a few yards before taking the steps on the left, back down to the river. Here you can see the remains of an old mill, complete with weir, mill pond, sluices and mill race.

Follow the footpath round over the bridge and back up to rejoin the track. Continue along the track past the mill buildings, and turn left at the last house. This is a paved way just before the road which, though it looks private, is in fact a public right of way.

At the bridge, you can see a weir which once helped to power the old paper mill. Over the bridge, swing right up an enclosed lane into Spa Woods. Follow the path to the end of the wall; a few yards further on, take the left fork down to a gate, then through a second gate to Spa Bridge. The bridge and woods

take their name from a nearby spring which once attracted large numbers of people here, hoping to benefit from its curative properties.

At Spa Bridge go over the stile and down the steps to continue along the riverside to Clough Foot Bridge. Turn left and take the gate on your right to continue down the valley. The path joins a track to Dauber Bridge. This is the original toll house of the old turnpike road up Cragg Vale, which linked Mytholmroyd and the Calder Valley to the Halifax-Rochdale turnpike at Blackstone Edge.

The turnpike road was given Royal Assent in 1815 and follows almost the same line as the present road. The Turnpike Trust was only wound up in 1886. These trusts generally continued until all the debts had been paid off from the tolls, and it took longer to complete this process in Cragg Vale than for either the Calder Valley or Blackstone Edge roads.

The Dauber Bridge Toll House has been enlarged, but the outine of the original building is still obvious. Note the two windows that remain on the bottom side, through which the toll-keeper could watch for approaching traffic.

Cross the road and turn right, before climbing up some steep stone steps. At the stile turn left, following the wall along the edge of the woods, crossing three fields. Go over the next stile and turn left to follow the path through the woods. This path narrows into an enclosed way before emerging into a small back road. Continue straight ahead, swinging left down Scout Road and past the Methodist Chapel, before turning right to the railway arch and the station. ❏

14. Luddenden Dean from Mytholmroyd

*An 8-mile (15km) walk over bracing
moorland and along a beautiful and secluded
valley*

WALK into Mytholmroyd by bearing right as you leave the railway station. Cross both the river and the main road, to pick up the canal towpath. Walk along it to the right: that is, in the direction of Halifax. At first you see little more than the backs of industrial units, but soon you emerge into open country. The first bridge you encounter is a new one; walk up and over it to rejoin the towpath.

Leave the towpath at the next bridge, at Brearley, and walk right along Halifax Road past houses and the Grove Inn. Immediately after the pub, bear slightly left up a cobbled track which leads you into Brearley Woods. After a few yards bear left, uphill. A number of paths climb through the woods, but you won't go wrong if you carry on walking uphill.

You will emerge from the woodland into Midgley; turn right along the road through the village. Just before the Sportsman pub, turn left up a cobbled track, waymarked "Link path to Calderdale Way". As the track forks, keep left towards a farmhouse. Past the house, go left up steps and across a field to a row of terraced houses. Keep left of the houses and go through a couple of stiles; continue in the same direction uphill.

Climb, keeping a field wall to your left. Squeeze through a gap in a tall field wall. At the next farm, keep to the right of the buildings. Over a stile you now meet the Calderdale Way, which here is a level grassy track at the edge of moorland. Go right along it to follow a wall, with views of Luddenden Foot extending down to the right.

The path soon swings to the left; you leave the open moorland via a stile on the right. Join a stony track bearing downhill, which soon becomes a concrete road. At the bottom you join a tarmac road and walk right, downhill; soon the road makes an acute hairpin bend to the right. About 100 yards past a farmhouse, go left, through a little gate, on a path waymarked "Jerusalem Farm". Descend through woodland to reach Wade Bridge — recently renovated — over Luddenden Brook.

Turn right over the bridge, to take a path that climbs through delightful oak woodland, keeping parallel to the brook. On the opposite side of the water is a picnic site that's very popular during the summer months. After about 500 yards of woodland walking, you come to a T-junction of well-defined tracks. Go left here; to guide you, there are wooden posts with tops painted yellow. After 50 yards you find yourself in a clearing, by a pool.

Keep to the right of the water, cross over a footbridge and immediately take a set of steps to the left, which begin by the gnarled roots of an old tree. At the top of the steps, go left along a tarmac track, but only for a few yards, until you go right, up more steps, through a gap

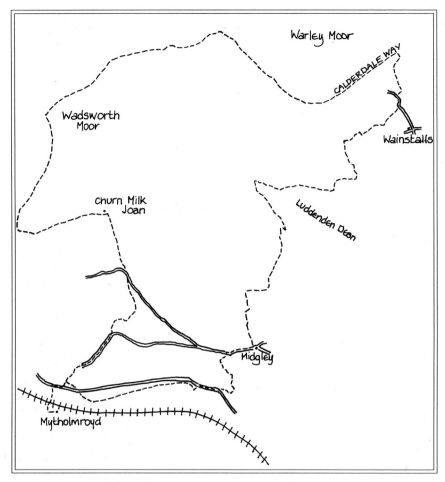

stile and onto a road.

Walk left along the road; very soon you approach terraced houses. Take a track to the left, immediately after the last house, and walk downhill towards an old mill pond. Cross a little stone bridge by a cottage, and walk through woodland for a few yards. Go through a gap in the fence ahead to follow a line of steps uphill, alongside a wall. If you look back from here, you will see the old mill that once was powered by water from the pond.

Beyond a gap stile in a wall, the path bears slightly left across a field to another wall. Follow the wall to the right, uphill, towards a little group of old houses; this is Lower Saltonstall. Go right as you meet the road; a mere 100 yards ahead is the Cat i' th' Well pub, very popular at weekends — not least because of its beer garden and children's playground.

Carry on, past the pub and across Cat Well Bridge that spans a little brook. Immediately after the bridge, take a set of steps — complete with iron hand-rail — climbing up to the left. Go through a little gate at the top; the path ahead is clear. When the track goes between walls, your way is to the right, up steps and then accompanying a wall. This is a paved path, though most of the stones have disappeared beneath the grass.

Negotiate a little stile and go left along a stony track that soon becomes cobbled and then meets a road. To the left is an old mill; to the right is a little cluster of houses — and another mill — that comprise the hamlet of Wainstalls. Your way is left, along the road; after 100 yards you take a path to the right, opposite a line of houses called Bridge Terrace. The route is waymarked "Link Path", because it links up with the Calderdale Way.

Walk up this engineered path as it becomes a causeway. Go left at a wall — the path is still paved — towards Moorfield Farm. Follow the causeway as it goes left of the farm buildings. Bear

right at a stile and big stone gateposts, as the causeway heads towards another farm. Over a stile, bear left along a stony track; after 50 yards you will see a sign to the left, informing you that the path you are now joining is part of the Calderdale Way.

Your route is now over the rough, unenclosed grazing land of Warley Moor; this is fine, level, breezy walking, with duckboards thoughtfully laid across the boggy areas of the path. The well-defined path descends to a road, crosses over and continues as a walled track ahead. Terrific views open up to your left, down the lovely valley of Luddenden Dean. When the Calderdale Way bears left, into the valley, you keep right to walk just to the right of a farm. Carry on, uphill, now on a tarmac track. Rejoin the road, and walk left along it. The road comes to an end at an eccentric building which comprises two

The Rochdale Canal at Brearley; walkers leave the towpath by this bridge and climb up onto Midgley Moor

castellated towers and an arched parapet slung between them.

Your waymarked path, however, is to be found just before the last house on the left. Cross the field ahead of you to a gate, and then carry straight down into the valley. The path soon becomes more

Take a path to the right of the "castle", waymarked "Public Footpath, Keelam Gate to Old Town". This path takes an uncompromisingly steep route up the valley; not a zig-zag in sight. You get a little breather in the middle, as the path levels off a bit, but the steep climb is then

An old cottage in the village of Midgley, which shows the narrow mullion windows that are so typical of Calderdale

distinct, and bears a little to the right. The last few yards down to the valley bottom are along a grassy track that descends in zig-zag fashion.

At the bottom, cross a stile by houses and walk along a tarmac road for a short way. Cross a beck to find yourself wondering if you are seeing double — for here is another castellated building, remarkably similar to the one you came across a few minutes ago. This building, however, is obviously of rather greater age. Both were built as gate-houses for the Castle Carr Estate.

resumed. You reach the top — eventually — as you clamber over an old wall onto a track heading to left and right. Your route, however, is straight ahead. You now leave bracken behind to cross open moorland. The path here is ill-defined, so just bear slightly to the left to pick up a track that follows a line of stone shooting butts, from which grouse and other game birds are sent to meet their maker. These butts will guide you unerringly over the moor.

As you leave the valley of Luddenden Dean behind, you go over the crest of a hill to get views down into another valley: that of the Calder valley containing Mytholmroyd and Hebden Bridge. Here on Wadsworth Moor you will probably be able to wander "lonely as a cloud", with just curlew or lapwing for company. Maybe you'll experience the heart-stopping moment when a covey of partridges takes off from beneath your feet with a whirr of wings.

When you reach a fence, you are once again joining the Calderdale Way. Go left to accompany the fence, keeping at a constant elevation. Walk along the edge of the moorland: heather to your left, valley stretching away to your right. As you cross a stile you are, albeit briefly, heading straight for Stoodley Pike, before wheeling left, around the shoulder of the hill.

It's a bit of a surprise to find yourself approaching a golf course; back to civilization indeed. A few yards beyond the clubhouse, the track forks. Bear left here, uphill. As you reach a stile, a sign points the way ahead: take the left path of two that converge here.

Keep just to the left of a fenced-off area of moor, to follow a wall. Pass an isolated barn and a couple of windswept trees beside it. Keep going, slightly uphill, until you reach the splendid six-foot boundary stone known as Churn Milk Joan. Turn right here, to accompany a wall downhill. Pass an old bread delivery van which has unaccountably decided to end its days here. The path is easy to follow and a little sign soon points the way down to Mytholmroyd, as you part company with the Calderdale Way.

Follow the wall downhill, cross a farm

A laithe-house in Luddenden Dean, which combines a barn and farmhouse under the same roof

track and then a stile, and then meet a road. Go left along it, but only until you reach a house to your right. Immediately past the house, pick up a path going steeply down to the right. It's a grassy path between walls — sunken in places. Keep just to the right of the track when it becomes boggy, and carry on down to join a track through woodland that emerges onto a road. Go right here, and back down into Mytholmroyd and the railway station. ❏

Left: Churn Milk Joan, a boundary stone standing alone in the heather of Midgley Moor

15. Sowerby Bridge to Littleborough

A 10-mile (18km) walk along the Ryburn Valley and over the famous causeway at Blackstone Edge

THE walk begins at the south side of Sowerby Bridge station; cross the station drive and enter the small park straight ahead via some steps. Walk round the bowling green and take the steps and zig-zagging path to the cottages above and to the right. Go down a cobbled lane in front of these cottages to a road, and turn left. From here there are superb views of the mills and terraced houses of Sowerby Bridge.

At the next junction continue right, downhill. Look for a lane branching off (Windsor Terrace) marked by a "No Through Road" sign. This lane contours along the hillside, providing a beautiful panorama over the Ryburn valley. Continue past a road junction; keep straight on at the next junction, down a lane marked "Wood Nook Only", to Lanes Bottom. Where the track swings left, take the stile and steps on the right through the wood, and down over a footbridge across the disused railway.

This is part of of the former double-track railway to Rishworth. The original proposal for the Ryburn branch, mooted in 1845, was to link Sowerby Bridge and Ripponden. A later and more ambitious plan was to create a main line from Rishworth, tunnelling under Blackstone Edge to join the Manchester-Leeds line near Hollingworth Lake.

Work began in 1873, but unexpected geological problems led to an increase in costs; finally, in 1881, the line was terminated permanently at Rishworth. The railway continued as a rural branch line between Sowerby Bridge and Rishworth, with "push and pull" passenger trains in operation until 1929. Freight trains used the line until 1958.

Drop down to the river opposite a mill and continue walking upstream until you join a cobbled lane at Triangle. There was a station here, also on the Rishworth branch. In 1905 Triangle was also directly linked to Halifax by electric tram; sadly this too disappeared many years ago.

Go left, back over the railway trackbed, bearing right down along a track. The track narrows after the cottages. Follow the line of old rotting posts that marks the path

through dense oak, birch and sycamore woods; at a stream drop down to the original trackbed. At the second railway bridge, turn left through a gap in the wall to join a stony track which eventually joins Old Bank dropping down into Ripponden.

This is a delightful Pennine town on the River Ryburn, with a fine Victorian church, a compact collection of cottages radiating along the hillsides and an ancient bridge. The present bridge dates from 1722 but it is almost certainly on the site of an earlier ford. The first stone bridge was built in 1533. Close by is a delightful white-washed building which used to be a pub, the Bridge Inn.

Ripponden was a important weaving centre and the Ryburn Valley was particularly famous for its dark "navy blue" cloth; at one time it was the sole supplier to the Royal Navy.

Unless you wish to explore the centre of Ripponden, don't cross the old packhorse bridge. Turn left, instead, just before this bridge, and go along the cobbled lane called Mill Fold. The lane goes under

Elland Road and emerges as a cindery track.

Walk straight ahead, joining a riverside path which passes a weir and mill race. At the footbridge turn sharp left up the steps and continue along a steep embankment to Whiteley's Hill car park. Turn right over the bridge and join the main road near Rishworth, famous for its school.

Cross the road to the bus stop bay on the other side, and take Bar Lane, signed to Ryburndale Paper Mill and Ripponden Trout Farm. This quiet lane follows the river past cottages and a mill pond (now serving as the trout farm) to the paper mill. Until recently, the mill made high quality paper for many purposes, including the printing of Bibles.

At the mill buildings, go directly ahead along the cobbled track which ascends under the arch (signed both "Private Road" and "Public Path"); keep ahead to where the track swings right. Your path is to the left of a double garage ahead, through a gateway at the front corner. This goes alongside buildings and joins a flight of steep steps up alongside Ryburn Reservoir Dam, emerging at a little car park.

Turn left across the dam, and then bear right at the end of the dam along a lovely waterside path through deciduous woodland. Ryburn Reservoir was built between 1925 and 1933 and holds 209 million gallons of water.

Cross the footbridge at the end of the reservoir, following a wooden sign towards New Barn and Heights. The path emerges above the wood at a stile. Keep alongside the field wall, following waymarks to the top of the field, before bearing left to New Barn Farm. Go through the gate near the farm, but follow the waymarks around the outside of the building to the top of the next field.

Turn left over a stile to a path along the top of the field to a gate, and join the track to Lower Wormald Farm ahead and a well-signed crosssing point of paths before the farmhouse. Take the path, right, to High Wormald, which goes through a narrow enclosed way, and stiles, into a field.

Walk diagonally across the field heading towards a waymarked stile in the wall ahead. Keep in the same direction across the next field with a signpost in the wall corner, to join an enclosed green track. Follow this track left (ignoring a stile straight ahead) as it swings around a hillock to the remains of Height Farm: really a collection of ruined barns.

Keep ahead, through gates, along the track which curves first to the right and then sharp left to reach a stile into a lay-by and viewing point on the road across Baitings Reservoir. From here you get a magnificent view across the reservoir and down the Ryburn valley with its scattered farms.

The next section of the walk should only be attempted in clear weather. In the event of mist or very low cloud, walkers are recommended to turn right to join the A58 road (there are bus services along here) and to pick up the Blackstone Edge path at a map-reading of SE 990 184 — just before the pylons cross the road.

But if the weather is good, cross the road to a green track directly ahead; take the lower of two gates into a sunken, green way to a second gate. Go through here, the grassy track climbing until it reaches open moorland, with the drystone wall to the right. Follow this deep sunken way (or keep to the edge) and keep straight on, even when the path almost vanishes.

Walk parallel to the A58, which lies about 600 yards to your right, gradually gaining height over Rishworth Moor. Posts act as useful waymarks. Continue in the same direction for about half a mile, until what appears to be a beck contouring around the hillside is visible ahead. Make for it; this is a reservoir catchwater, Warm Withens Drain, and a faint path will be discernible alongside it. Follow it to the left; you have easy, level walking as it curves round to the left to meet Rishworth Drain. Turn right alongside the drain as it contours around a deep hollow, along which you may be able to pick out the Blackstone Edge path coming up from the A58: the bad weather alternative.

When you reach a footbridge at the crossing of paths, take the path to the left, waymarked "Roman Road and Pennine Way", over the footbridge. You are now on a broad sunken track, hidden under boggy cotton grass in places, but in other places revealed as a beautifully metalled road — the Blackstone Edge Causeway — in all its glory.

Follow the causeway steadily uphill until you reach the summit of the pass. Here you will find the Aiggin Stone, which acts as an unmistakable waymark on the top of Blackstone Edge. The official route of the Pennine Way also crosses at this point.

The Aiggin Stone is a magnificent column of gritstone, seven feet high and inscribed with a cross. It was a medieval guide stoop, and marks the county boundary. "Aiggin" is thought to derive from either of two French words: *aigulle* meaning needle or peak, or *aigle* meaning eagle.

The Aiggin Stone also marks the beginning of a superb section of drained pavement with a central channel. There has been much debate about the purpose of this trough. Some have argued that it was for drainage, while other

Cottages and the old bridge over the River Ryburn at Ripponden, a small town once renowned for its "navy blue" cloth

experts have suggested that it was filled with turf to give a better foothold for horses labouring up the steep gradient. Less contentious, however, are the breath-taking views of the Lancashire plain, with its chimneys and mills — recalling Lowry paintings — that still dominate the landscape.

Blackstone Edge possibly derives its name from the gritstone crags which rise to 1475ft on its summit. The word "black" in the Pennines often denotes a border — in this case the one between Lancashire and Yorkshire.

The journey over the top has been chronicled by many travellers, including Celia Fiennes, who described Blackstone Edge in her diary of 1698 as a "dismal high precipice steep in ascent" with "moorish ground all about". Da-

niel Defoe crossed the Edge in August 1724, during a blizzard that was unseasonal even for the Pennines. Not surprisingly Defoe declared that "the depth of the precipice and narrowness of the way looked horrid to us".

This ancient highway is mentioned in various medieval texts. The Calandar of Patent Rolls (1291) refers to it as Blakesteynegge, which is one reason why many historians have assumed it to be of Roman origin.

It has been suggested that the road formed part of a route between the forts of Manchester (Mancunium) and Ilkley (Olicana) in Yorkshire. Indeed, the arm of a silver statuette — inscribed with a dedication to Valerius Rufus of the Sixth Legion — was found near Hollingworth Lake. In Britain from 120 AD, the Sixth

Walkers with a head for heights can walk along the top of the dam which holds back the waters of Baitings Reservoir

Legion was stationed in Ribchester, Hadrian's Wall, York, Manchester and Melandra.

This theory was questioned by the late James Maxim, who pointed out the closeness of the proven Roman highway between Manchester and York through the Colne Valley, via Slack and Castleshaw. Maxim argued that the road over Blackstone Edge was actually a pre-turnpike packhorse way. He thought its construction resembled a Pennine causeway more than a public or campaigning road from Roman times.

Those historians convinced that the road is indeed Roman have pointed to research done in the 1920s, which revealed a Roman road from Moston (a suburb of Manchester) towards what is now Milnrow. Furthermore, there is a Roman road at Royton. Archaeological excavations in Manchester increasingly

suggest that Mancunium was an important Roman manufacturing centre. It would therefore be no surprise to find the Roman road network more complex than previously thought. Arguments will no doubt continue to rage about the origins of this fascinating road.

Carry on down the road almost to the parking place on the A58, but veer off left before it onto a narrow path. You continue along another ancient road, though this one is now less obvious and without any trace of pavement. Keep alongside the field wall, crossing a shallow ravine to Lydgate. Bear right at the cottages to the road.

Not far past the cottages is a ruined farmhouse. At one time it was a packhorse inn, and close by is a drinking trough for the use of pack-ponies. They travelled in long trains of 20-30 beasts — their panniers loaded with raw materi-

This beautifully engineered road descends steeply down Blackstone Edge, and continues to inspire controversy about its origins

als or finished products — between the markets of Lancashire and Yorkshire.

Follow the lane left for about 100 yards before turning left through a gate on a waymarked field-path; it bears half left towards the corner of the field where there is a stile in the wall. Turn right along the far side of the wall over a series of stiles, until the path drops to a stile in the wall corner and crosses a stream.

Cross another stile to the edge of a restored cottage, Owlet Hall. Opposite the cottage garden gate is a tall gate with an arch, on the right. Go through this gate, onto a narrow path down into a little ravine below the golf course, with signs of former coal mining activity, through the scattered trees of Ealees Wood.

The path zig-zags down to join a tar-mac track by a stream in the Ealees valley. Turn right (ignoring the waymark indicating left) along the lane which leads into Ealees. You pass the old weaving cottages and a mill that dates from the mid-18th century. It was here, in the late 1940s, that Tygan, a woven plastic cloth, was developed as a replacement for deck-chair canvas.

Continue along the street, cross over the Rochdale Canal and turn left into Littleborough town centre and the railway station. You can reach Littleborough Heritage Centre in the Old Coach House by crossing a newly pedestrianised little square. In the centre are displays which reveal much about the history of Littleborough and the surrounding area. ❑

16. Norland Moor from Sowerby Bridge

A 7-mile (13km) tour of typical Calderdale country, finishing off with a bracing ridge-top walk

AS you stand outside Sowerby Bridge station you see a steep slope ahead of you. The walk begins by climbing this slope, so walk to the right and then head up left, past a bowling green. Pick up a path that makes the gradual ascent of Allen Park by zig-zagging, or take the more direct approach by climbing the steps.

Either way you will soon be at the top of the slope; towards the right is a little row of terraced houses. Bear left here, along a path that veers uphill along the far side of a cast-iron fence. As you climb you will get ever more expansive views back down over Sowerby Bridge, and further east towards Halifax and that magnificent folly, Wainhouse Tower.

Where the fence ends, you continue along a paved pathway, directly uphill now. As you pass a couple of houses, the path brings you out onto a road. Walk left, in the direction of Wainhouse Tower, but only for a few yards till you go through a gap-stile on the right. From here a path bears left to cross over a field. The presence of cobbles, and slight engineering to make a level track despite the slope, lets you know that this is yet another paved causeway.

Squeeze through another gap-stile, and follow the line of the causey — even though many of the flags have now disappeared beneath the grass of this pasture. At the top of the field, turn left at a wall, to arrive at a stile in the corner of the field. Turn up right here, along the edge of the field.

The top edge of the field is defined by big slabs of stone, each one set on end in the ground to form a wall of great permanence. These are known in some areas as "vaccary" walls, the best-known examples probably being those at Wycoller, to the north-west of Calderdale. These walls were used to construct enclosures for dairy cattle, and many are of great age.

Follow this strange wall to the left, along another section of causeway. Go through a stile, then head across a field to another stile just to the left of the Blue Ball Inn.

Cross a little road here, and take an enclosed track straight ahead, with a "footpath" sign. Keep along this track, then forward along the edge of a field to a cluster of buildings, walking straight ahead when you get to a very minor road. At another collection of buildings, carry straight on over a little crossroads along an even more minor road across moorland.

When you reach another road, keep left along it, but only for a few yards. You leave the road along a track going left in front of a bungalow. This grassy track forms part of the Calderdale Way. To the left is a wooded clough; you are walking along the top edge of it. After some pleasant, easy walking you begin to descend, as the path accompanies a fence to the left. Cross a stile to go into oak woods. When you see a house on

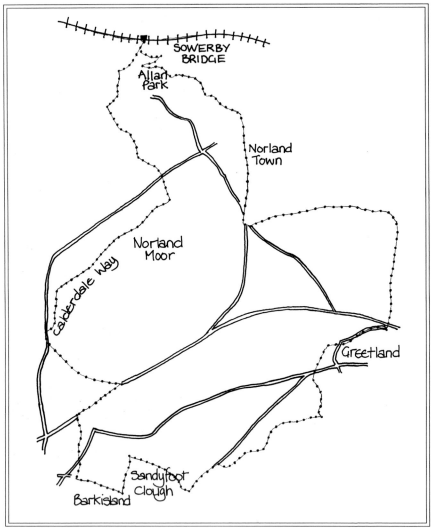

the right, you meet a woodland track. Keep the same direction and follow the track, as the Calderdale Way soon bears off to the left.

At a crossing of tracks, carry straight on in the direction of an electricity pylon. Pass the Old Vicarage down to the main road. Cross the road and take Brian Royd Lane, going down to the right. When you reach a junction with the rather painful-sounding Scar Bottom Lane, you keep straight on to join a pleasant enclosed track. Keep left when the track forks and walk down to the main road by the Branch Road Inn.

Cross the road and take a little enclosed path that runs just to the left of the pub. Go through a metal gate and, a few yards further on, go left through a gap-stile to follow the edge of a field to another gap-stile. After the stile, go right to enter woodland. Descend to a tarmac track, and go right towards an old mill. Just before you get to the mill, however, take a path to the right to follow the bank of a little beck. Go through a stile constructed from surplus ironmongery, and keep the beck company through a couple of kissing gates. Soon you find you are on a paved path, as you approach another mill, though this one hums with activity.

Your way is between the extensive mill buildings, passing to the right of a chimney, to reach a road. Go left along the road for about 500 yards; on the left you will see some new houses built in a style that, for once, seems to blend in successfully with the older vernacular architecture of Calderdale.

Look out for a gap-stile on the right, immediately after a house standing on its own. Take this path, uphill, way-marked "Sandyfoot Clough". Follow the house wall, then bear half-right across the field to pick up a gate in the far right-hand corner. You now have pleasant walking along the clough, with the little beck to your right. You leave the clough at a wooden stile; from here you walk left, follow a field wall, and pass by a small brick-built enclosure. Carry straight on along a walled track, to reach a fine old house, Barkisland Hall.

Go right along the road into the little village of Barkisland. There are a few interesting houses in the village, including one with a splendid old porch dated 1618. Turn right, soon, up Stoney Butts Lane; beyond the houses you carry on along an enclosed path to the road. Cross the road and take a path that runs along the back of the Northfield pub.

You negotiate stone stiles before you

These old and distinctive enclosures, made from stone slabs set on end in the ground, are often known as vaccary walls

reach a road. Go right here for about 200 yards, and then take a path to the left, just past a farm. Your route is way-marked "Norland via Gallow's Pole Hill". Cross a farm track and head

thrown from here during the Middle Ages. Scramble up the rock to enjoy the view.

Amongst the names, dates and expressions of undying love carved into

The distinctive profile of Ladstone Rock looks down from Norland Moor over Sowerby Bridge and the Ryburn Valley.

straight uphill on another track. Keep left of woodland to emerge onto a breezy hill-top — this is Gallow's Pole Hill, no less — which offers a splendidly agricultural vista over farms and fields divided up by dry-stone walls.

Follow the shoulder of the hill to the right, to meet a road, albeit briefly. After only 100 yards, go right to accompany the Calderdale Way along a sandy track. The track climbs along the edge of Norland Moor, giving extensive views over Ripponden and the Ryburn valley. A triangulation point is soon revealed to the right, while on your left is the craggy outcrop known as Ladstone Rock. Legend has it that convicted witches were

the rock is a metal plaque, inscribed thus, with one of the psalms:

Sing to God,
Sing praises to His name;
Lift up a song to Him
Who rides upon
the clouds;
His name is the Lord,
Exult before Him.

Keep walking on this sandy track along the rocky ridge. Soon you will be able to see Wainhouse Tower once again, and Sowerby Bridge. The pits and hollows in this area tell of old quarrying. There are a number of tracks criss-crossing this part of Norland Moor; it's a popular place for local people to exercise their dogs and enjoy a bracing stroll. There are plenty of paths, too, which descend into the valley; your best route is to take a track about 100 yards past a solitary house you can see below you, which has a square, walled garden.

At a road, go right for a few yards and then left on a path waymarked "Sowerby Bridge". You go beneath a little bridge provided for the convenience of people playing on the Ryburn Golf Course. You pass the golf club: it's not every course whose clubhouse is a splendid old building with mullioned windows.

From the clubhouse your way is down a tarmac track, turning right as you reach a road. When you meet another road, by a row of terraced houses which enjoy fine views of Sowerby Bridge, go left for just 30 yards. Go right, just before another house, down a pathway with a trio of iron bollards at the top. For much of its length, this path is setted, until it becomes tarmaced and meets a road. Bear right here, and then keep left as the roads fork, to get back into Sowerby Bridge. ❏

17. Halifax Town Trail

*A tour around a town built on civic pride
and the wool trade, ending with the
magnificent Piece Hall*

SET among the Pennine Hills, Halifax was a town in the vanguard of the Industrial Revolution. Its splendid buildings — Victorian and earlier — reflect the town's status in the textile industry, though wool had brought prosperity from the Middle Ages onwards. By 1572 there was certainly a cloth hall here, to which merchants would come to sell their lengths of cloth.

The "cottage industry" of hand-weaving and spinning declined as the mills began to dominate the valley, bringing prosperity to the few and long hours and hard labour to many. Families such as the Crossleys (of carpet fame) were responsible for erecting many of the town's finest buildings, and "the Halifax" is indisputably the largest building society in the world.

Much of the centre of Halifax has been modernised, yet there are still plenty of interesting buildings to be seen, whose past is rooted in the days of the Industrial Revolution.

Walk out along the station concourse, and turn right at the traffic lights. The prominent landmarks, as you cross the road, are a pair of churches; both were once splendid buildings, though their recent history has been chequered.

Square Chapel (named after this particular part of town, and not from the shape of the building) was built in the Palladian style and opened in 1772. It is one of the few brick buildings in Calderdale that date from this period. Now the windows are boarded up and "Keep Out" notices merely emphasise the chapel's neglected appearance. However, plans are in hand for its renovation.

Next to it is Square Church, built in 1857, largely with funds donated by the Crossley family. The church once accommodated as many as 1,200 parishioners, but a fire in 1971 destroyed most of the building except for the spire. This tall, slender and elegant landmark was consolidated and cleaned seven years later.

A few yards further up the road is the Calderdale Industrial Museum, housed in the four storeys of what was once a warehouse. Here you can get a real feel of what it was like to live and work in industrial Halifax. More than 20 local industries are represented. You can see giant steam engines at work, and crouch in the claustrophobic shadows of a coal mine. There is a large collection of machinery related to the town's textile trade, and other industries with local associations, such as Macintosh's toffees and Crossley Carpets.

Having looked around the museum, cross the road again. Go down Alfred Street East, and then left to arrive at the 500-year-old parish church: a soot-blackened edifice, in contrast to the light-coloured and sand-blasted buildings in the vicinity. Across the road is a pub called, appropriately, the Ring O'Bells.

From the church, walk up Causeway and cross to the unprepossessing façade of the main car park. Climb a flight of steps ahead of you, and walk across the carpark to Sainsbury's and other new

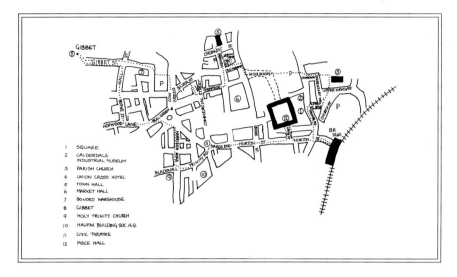

1   SQUARE
2   CALDERDALE
    INDUSTRIAL MUSEUM
3   PARISH CHURCH
4   UNION CROSS HOTEL
5   TOWN HALL
6   MARKET HALL
7   BONDED WAREHOUSE
8   GIBBET
9   HOLY TRINITY CHURCH
10 HALIFAX BUILDING SOC. H.Q.
11 CIVIC THEATRE
12 PIECE HALL

shops. This area — known as Wool-shops — was redeveloped in the mid-80s.

A timber-framed building on the top corner has been retained, though the "improvements" have made the building look more like a pastiche than the original it actually is.

Go right, then first left for a few yards, up Old Market. On the right is the Union Cross Hotel; it was first mentioned in 1535 and thus qualifies as the oldest inn in the town centre. For many years it enjoyed a rather insalubrious reputation, with cock-fighting a regular "entertainment". Later, the pub was a staging post for coach travellers.

Walk through an archway just to the right of the pub entrance; it becomes a ginnel which, after a left turn, deposits you onto Princess Street. This street, and others in this part of town, was the creation of John Crossley, one of the brothers who were responsible for making Crossley Carpets such a successful concern.

The many fine buildings in Princess Street, built during the middle of the 19th century, exhibit some of the stylis-tic decorations of which our Victorian forebears were so proud.

Go right along Princess Street to Crossley Street and investigate the Town Hall, of similar age, and designed by Sir Charles Barry, whose principal claim to fame was as the architect responsible for the Houses of Parliament. No stone, it seems, was left uncarved, and no opportunity spared to add ornamentation. Here is civic pride made visible.

Retrace your steps along Princess Street and carry on to the next road on the left. Opposite you is the market building, which you enter through a big archway. The whole building — the market itself and the shops that surround it on all sides — were built, in 1896, as a unified scheme. The market remains both a splendid building, with a ceiling of decorated ironwork and glass, as well as a characterful and noisy place of trade.

In short, it's a proper market, with household requisites of every kind "piled high and sold cheap" in traditional manner, with their virtues extolled, without false modesty, by voluble stall-holders. What a pity that too many markets these days are soulless places, where traders aren't encouraged to raise their voices above conversational level.

Leave the market at the opposite end to where you came in; you emerge into Albion Street. Go right and right again, along South Gate — now a pedestrian precinct. Take the first road on the left, also signalled as being for "pedestrians only". This is Old Cock Yard, though the pub that gave the yard its name is now closed down. At the top of this short road is Lloyds Bank, on Commercial Street. This building—and others nearby — are fine examples of Victorian architecture.

To the right of Lloyds Bank is George Street; here you will find Somerset House, a splendid Georgian building built in 1766 as a home for John Royds, a banker. Unfortunately, much of the frontage is now hidden by shops.

Walk up George Street to the top and then head right along Cow Green. Go left up a flight of steps immediately before a pub called, with mirthless humour, "Hangovers". Turn right at the top of the steps and follow a road round to the left.

Soon you will see, on your left, the Bonded Warehouse. It was built to store goods on which duty had not yet been paid; the storage of such good was under the jurisprudence of Customs and Excise. Halifax was one of the first inland towns to have such a bonded warehouse. Now the building serves a different role: as an electrical wholesaler.

Carry on walking up Gibbet street; cross the dual carriageway of Burdock Lane to arrive at the Halifax Gibbet. As fearsome as this "guillotine" looks, only the site is genuine.

It was at this spot that petty thieves were sent to meet their maker. In the Middle Ages the Lord of the Manor was entitled to execute anyone caught stealing goods with a value of a shilling or more. In most areas of the country, this practice died out during the 14th century. In Halifax, however, miscreants' heads were still being parted from their bodies until 1650.

After this date the executioner was laid off, and the gibbet became no more than a footnote in the history of Halifax. The original blade is now displayed in the Pre-Industrial Museum, which is housed in the Piece Hall. The gibbet on display now is a faithful, but inoperative, replica.

Retrace your steps back over Burdock Way, and turn right in front of the Bonded Warehouse. Pass the Elim Pentecostal Church, a modern place of worship, and continue along Boyne Street. Turn left at the end, into Hopwood Lane. On your left is Hopwood Hall: a handsome Georgian town house.

Cross the road at the traffic lights and go right around the roundabout to turn off at Harrison Road, a street blessed with some fine buildings from the Georgian and Victorian periods. Pass the former Police Station (now Magistrates' Courts), and then Holy Trinity Church.

Turn left opposite the church, down Trinity Road, to come across the town's most remarkable modern building — the headquarters of the Halifax Building Society. It was built in 1972-4 and its uncompromising design reinforces the Halifax's position as the biggest building society in the world. The building has elicited plaudits from some quarters (including the RIBA) and derision from others. It is certainly distinctive.

At the crossroads, look left to see the Civic Theatre, which opened in 1901 with a rendition of Beethoven's Funeral March to honour the memory of the late Queen Victoria. Walk downhill; on the

Right: A faithful replica of the infamous Halifax Gibbet, used to execute petty criminals until 1650

The collonades of the Piece Hall surround a huge courtyard, which is now used for markets, concerts and other public events

right is Holly House. The centre section was built in 1755, and the wings were later additions. It is now a pub. Carry on down Horton Street, and turn left along Cross Street to enter the last — and most interesting — port of call.

It's hard to believe that only a few years ago the Piece Hall was in danger of being demolished. Fortunately — for Halifax and for us — this barbarous notion got no further. For the Piece Hall is a marvellous building and a fitting monument to a pre-industrial trade.

Your first reaction, as you enter the vast central courtyard, may well be surprise—at finding yourself in a building that would not look out of place in Renaissance Italy. And yet this monumental building was established for a very down-to-earth purpose: as a market place for the cloth produced by local weavers. The name of the building derives from these lengths of hand-woven cloth, which were known as "pieces".

Because of the sloping site, there are three levels on the bottom side and two at the top. Each collonaded level is built in a different classical style, with Doric columns, archways and squared-off "rustic" supports. The courtyard enclosed by the collonades is massive — about 10,000 square yards.

The Piece Hall was built in 1779, many years before the advent of the mills and mechanised weaving. At this date, weaving was still a cottage industry, and the Piece Hall's 315 rooms were used by the hand-weavers of the district to promote their wares. The customers were dealers from all over the country, and even agents acting for dealers overseas.

The mechanisation of the weaving process towards the middle of the last century left the Piece Hall sadly redundant. In the intervening years it has served a variety of purposes, including a venue for political orations and — for over a century — a wholesale market.

The building was cleaned, renovated and given a new lease of life in the 1970s. Today, the rooms are rented to small businesses, including artists and craftspeople. Visitors can wander along the arcades and find original gifts; there can surely be few shopping areas housed in such beautiful surroundings.

The Tourist Information Centre is adjacent to the gate by which you entered. There are markets here every Friday and Saturday, flea-markets on Thursdays, and the courtyard is the venue for a great many special events, including concerts and exhibitions. To complement the Calderdale Industrial Museum next door, the Piece Hall houses a pre-industrial museum, which tells the story of textile manufacture in Calderdale before the Industrial Revolution changed Pennine life for ever.

There is an art gallery, too, which features work by local artists and takes travelling exhibitions from all over the country.

Halifax, having recognised the Piece Hall's uniqueness, has made a great success of promoting it as an attraction for visitors.

Despite the many uses to which the Piece Hall is put, it happily retains a lot of the atmosphere associated with its long and distinguished history.

If you leave the Piece Hall via Cross Street, you should turn left down Horton Street to arrive back at the railway station. ❏

Above: A detail from one of the iron doors of the Piece Hall, built in 1779 as a market in which "pieces" of cloth were bought and sold.

18. Magna Via and Shibden Hall

A 5-mile (9km) walk from Halifax along an old packhorse route, calling at a fascinating 15th century hall and museum

LEAVE Halifax railway station and turn right at the traffic lights. Walk down Church Street to the smoke-blackened parish church. Bear left past the church, along Lower Kirkgate, and then right down Bank Bottom to cross Hebble Brook.

Walk uphill to where the road makes a very sharp left-hand bend, at which point you walk straight ahead up a steep cobbled track, which climbs to join Beacon Hill road. Turn right here; after 200 yards cross the road and take a way-marked path uphill. By the road is a metal plaque which tells you a little about the history of this track, known as the Magna Via — Latin for "Great Way".

For centuries this route provided the only practicable approach to Halifax from the east, for both foot and packhorse traffic. The Magna Via became particularly important as the textile trade began to flourish in the Calder valley. Packhorse trains would bring in wool, and take away the finished lengths of cloth. The Magna Via remained the principal route to the east until 1741, when a turnpike road was built. It took a longer route to the north of the old Magna Via, in order to provide a less precipitous gradient more suitable for wheeled traffic.

Eighty years later another turnpike road, which was to become the present A58 road, was built; it flattened out the gradients even more. The old Magna Via, now surplus to travelling requirements, was left undisturbed to revert to nature.

From the metal plaque you follow this delightful cobbled path as it leads steeply uphill, offering increasingly

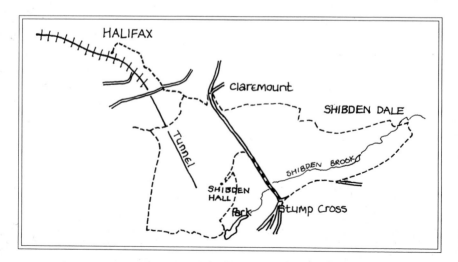

The cobbles of the Magna Via — an old pack-horse route — climb steeply out of Halifax towards the heights of Beacon Hill

extensive views of Halifax spread out below. At a left-hand hairpin bend the full width of the track has been excavated, to give an idea of how it must have looked when the heavily laden pack-ponies came this way. Carry on climbing until you reach a "footpath" sign. Make a detour here by taking the steep path which heads off to the right; it takes you to the top of Beacon Hill, from which the views will be stunning — on a clear day at least.

Beacon Hill looks down on the town from a height of about 400 feet: high enough to give the railway line, station and the town stretched out behind the appearance of a giant model railway layout. Even the bulk of Dean Clough Mill appears diminutive as you gaze down.

If you have already completed the Halifax town trail (Walk 17) then you will be able to put names to many of the notable buildings that claim your attention, even from the heights of Beacon Hill. There's the Piece Hall; it's hard to believe, in these heritage-conscious 90s, that this magnificent 18th century monument to the town's textile industry was saved from the bulldozer only at the eleventh hour.

Fronting the Piece Hall is the needle-sharp spire of the Square Congregational Church, rising 235 feet into the sky; the church itself was destroyed by fire in 1971, but the spire - amazingly - survived.

A more modern landmark, to the left, is the new headquarters of the Halifax Building Society. This extravagant building, in a diamond shape, reflects the status of the world's largest building society.

The vantage point of Beacon Hill used to have an important role in the defence of these islands. It was one of the summits on which beacons were lit to warn of the approach of the Spanish Armada in 1588. Early illustrations show an iron container, set on top of a pole, in which the fire could be lit. The beacon has been lit in earnest on at least two other occasions: in 1688 to announce the landing of William of Orange, and in 1745 to warn the population about the invading army from Scotland. In more recent years, the flames have risen up from Beacon Hill on more celebratory occasions such as jubilees, coronations and — most joyfully of all — at the cessation of war.

Retrace your steps, but only as far as the footpath sign; rejoin the Magna Via as it bears to the right. The panorama of Halifax recedes, to be replaced by extensive views into the Shibden valley. When you reach a giant retaining wall — a relic of old quarry workings — you have a choice of unmade roads. To the right is a track called Long Lane; but the track you want is Barraclough Lane, ahead — a wide track that has its own flagged causeway down one side for use by pedestrians.

Pass Marsh Delph Lane, which comes in from the right; a few yards further on is a gate across your track. Just before the gate is an enclosed path that leads down to the left. This is Pump Lane — though there is no sign to tell you as much — and it takes you straight down into the valley.

The path is sunken — with fields to the height of the walls on left and right. At the bottom of Pump Lane you have to weave between a clutch of new houses to reach a road. Across the road is Rodridge Farm; just to the right of the farm entrance is a small iron gate and a narrow paved path that runs between

Left: Beacon Hill offers a splendid panoramic view over Halifax; the Piece Hall and the spire of Square Congregational Church are prominent

From the Magna Via, the view extends past the air-shafts of the railway tunnel into Shibden Dale

fields. Take this track; it leads directly into Shibden Park alongside the childrens' playground and the boating lake — an animated scene during the summer months.

Make your way through this pleasant parkland by following the tarmac road until you see a sign on the left: "Footpath to Shibden Hall". Take this path through trees and along a little paved path to arrive at Shibden Hall, a splendid house which dates back to 1420. As is often the case with houses of this age, it has undergone a number of alterations and additions in the intervening years. Nevertheless, the core of the original house remains. Don't begrudge the admission charge, as the hall is worth exploring inside as well as out.

The rooms are furnished in period style, to show how they might have looked over the five and a half centuries that Shibden Hall has been a family

home — for the Oates, Saviles, Waterhouses and, latterly, the Listers. Much use has been made of wood panelling: beautiful to look at, but how dark the rooms must have appeared during the long winter evenings, when candle-light was the only illumination. The wooden furniture has that patina of age that antique forgers strive in vain to emulate.

An adjacent barn and other outbuildings house a folk museum. There is a collection of vehicles — from a horse-drawn hearse to a "stop me and buy one" ice-cream vending trailer. You can see farm machinery and the tools of many trades in the workshops clustered around a courtyard: wheelwright, cooper (barrel-maker), blacksmith, saddler and potter. There is even an old pub, complete with spittoons.

Having admired both the hall and museum, retrace your steps along the paved path and through the woodland. Walk left towards the main road, but go right before you meet it. Walk along a little road past terraced houses; to the left is the tall retaining wall that was built to enable the main road from Halifax to Leeds and Bradford to maintain a more gentle gradient than the terrain would otherwise have allowed.

At the end of this little road, climb a set of well-worn stone steps to arrive on the road by the Museum pub. Cross the road and walk up Kell Lane — to the right of the Stump Cross Inn. After 500 yards a cobbled road joins the road at an acute angle; take a tarmac track here that bears away slightly to the left. The way ahead is clear—through a little gate and along a paved path. Now you can see down into Shibden Dale, a well-wooded valley.

Your way is through open pasture, then following a wall on your right. Soon the paved area extends to the width of a cart, and you can see the grooves worn in the stones by the wheels. After about half a mile of field walking, you reach a minor road. Turn left here to arrive very shortly at Shibden Mill Inn, a fine building of great age. Walk through the car park to the far end, where a bridleway called Horley Green Lane begins.

Walk up this track; as it levels out you find another double line of paving beneath your feet. All too soon the paving disappears; from here you walk along a cinder track. When it forks, keep right, uphill. Pass what is something of a rarity in these parts: a brick-built house.

The track becomes a sunken way, and then narrows to a footpath between walls. Carry on until you emerge among the houses of Claremount, to see Beacon Hill ahead of you. As you bear right, you find yourself directly above the A58, as it goes through a steep-sided cutting. This is Godley Cutting, built to replace Lister Road as the main route out of Halifax to the east. The depth of the cutting made the gradient less severe: a problem encountered for centuries by travellers along the Magna Via and, later, Lister Road.

Cross the cutting via a bridge, then walk down a set of steps immediately to the right. Walk left along a road, to pick up the route you took at the beginning of the walk. Retrace your steps from here back to Halifax station. ❑

USEFUL INFORMATION

TOURIST INFORMATION CENTRES

Rochdale TIC, Town Hall, Rochdale. Tel (0706) 356592

Hebden Bridge TIC, Bridge Gate, Hebden Bridge. Tel (0422) 843831

Halifax TIC, Piece Hall, Halifax. Tel (0422) 68725

Todmorden TIC, 15 Burnley Road, Todmorden. Tel (0706) 818181

RAILWAY STATIONS

To check on train times at the stations in Calderdale (Halifax, Sowerby Bridge, Mytholmroyd, Hebden Bridge, Todmorden and Walsden), telephone Bradford (0274) 733994. For Littleborough, Smithy Bridge and Rochdale stations, telephone 061 832 8353.

PLACES OF INTEREST

Calder Valley Cruising: Visitor Centre at Barge Branwell, The Marina, New Road, Hebden Bridge. Tel (0422) 844833

Piece Hall, Halifax. (Markets every Friday and Saturday). Tel (0422) 368725

Piece Hall Pre-Industrial Museum, Halifax. Tel (0422) 359031

Calderdale Industrial Museum, Halifax. Tel (0422) 359031

Shibden Hall Folk Museum, Halifax. Tel (0422) 352246

Automobilia, (Vintage Car Museum), Hebden Bridge. Tel (0422) 844775

Walkley's Clogs, near Hebden Bridge. Tel (0422) 842061

Hardcastle Crags, near Hebden Bridge. Tel (0422) 844518

Childhood Reflections (toy museum), Hebden Bridge. Tel (0422) 845558

Hollingworth Lake Country Park, near Rochdale. Tel (0706) 73421

Pioneers Co-operative Museum, Rochdale. Tel (0706) 524920

Littleborough Coach House (heritage and information centre). Tel (0706) 78481

GUIDED WALKS (free, no need to book in advance) taking in many different landscapes and themes: explaining about birds, wild flowers, sheep-shearing, coiners, etc. To find out more, telephone The Calderdale Countryside Service, (0422) 359454, ext 248 or 233. For details of guided walks in the Rochdale area, telephone (0706) 73421

ORGANISATIONS

The British Trust for Conservation Volunteers does a great deal of valuable work; you can contact the South Pennine branch on 061 762 9075.

The South Pennines Association; contact the secretary on 061 665 3536.

Pennine Heritage (and *Pennine* magazine), the Birchcliffe Centre, Hebden Bridge.

The Rochdale Canal Countryside Management Project. Tel (0422) 844990.

Mankinholes Youth Hostel, Tel (0706) 812340

BOOKS

On the Tops around Todmorden, by Geoff Boswell, published by Delta G, £3.50.

Pennine Walks around Hebden Bridge, published by Calder Civic Trust, £3.45.

Walks in Calderdale, by Paul Hannon, published by Hillside Publications, £2.45.

Calderdale Architecture and History, published by Ryburn Publishing, £6.95. (Superb photography).

Fabric of the Hills, by Elizabeth Jane Pridmore, published by SCOSPA (Standing Conference of South Pennine Authorities) £3.95.

The Manchester & Leeds Railway, written and published by Martin Bairstow, £4.95.

19th Century Halifax Travel & Transport, by Eric Webster, published by H Greenwood & Sons, £1.75.

A number of excellent little-booklets about the South Pennines (covering architecture, hand-weaving, the industrial revolution, the coming of the railway and canal, the making of the Pennine landscape etc) are published by Pennine Heritage in Hebden Bridge. These and many other publications are available from TICs.

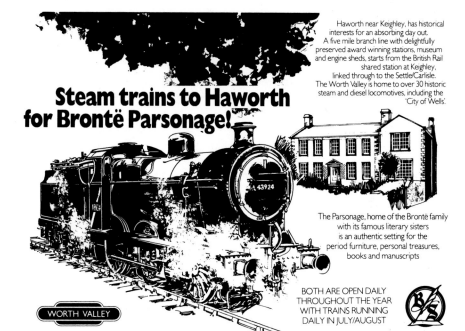

Steam trains to Haworth for Brontë Parsonage!

Haworth near Keighley, has historical interests for an absorbing day out. A five mile branch line with delightfully preserved award winning stations, museum and engine sheds, starts from the British Rail shared station at Keighley, linked through to the Settle/Carlisle. The Worth Valley is home to over 30 historic steam and diesel locomotives, including the 'City of Wells'.

The Parsonage, home of the Brontë family with its famous literary sisters is an authentic setting for the period furniture, personal treasures, books and manuscripts

BOTH ARE OPEN DAILY THROUGHOUT THE YEAR WITH TRAINS RUNNING DAILY IN JULY/AUGUST

WORTH VALLEY

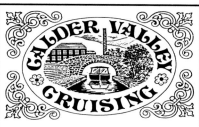

Mail order books from Leading Edge

Other titles on the **RailTrail** theme

The Isle of Man by Tram, Train and Foot — *Stan Basnett and David Freke, £4.95*

The Great Metro Guide to Tyne and Wear — *Vernon Abbott and Roy Chapman,* £5.95

Settle & Carlisle Country, featuring a new walkers' and cyclists' route from Leeds to Carlisle — *Colin Speakman and John Morrison, £5.95*

Exploring Strathclyde by Rail— *Tom Noble, £5.75*

Buxton Spa Rail Rambles — *Les Lumsdon and Martin Smith,* 99p

Stockton on Tees: Birthplace of Railways — *Lydia Speakman and Roy Chapman,* £1.95

Other railway books

The Line that Refused to Die — *Stan Abbott and Alan Whitehouse tell the story of the successful campaign to save the Settle & Carlisle line. Features a foreword by Michael Palin. £6.25 in paperback. Commemorative hardback edition, £13.50.*

The Wensleydale Railway — *Christine Hallas, £3.25*

To Kill a Railway — *Stan Abbott's historic account of British Rail's attempts to close the Settle & Carlisle line, £3.95*

Other outdoor books

The Off-Road Bicycle Book. *Second edition of Iain Lynn's authoritative run-down on mountain biking, £4.95*

The Birds of Lincolnshire and South Humberside — *Stephen Lorand and Keith Atkin, £12.50*

Brick by Brick, *guide to building your own home, £6.25*

All available from your bookshop or direct from —
Leading Edge, Old Chapel, Burtersett, Hawes,
North Yorkshire, DL8 3PB.
Use our telephone credit card ordering service, or write or phone for our up-to-date catalogue.

Postage and packing charges — books under £2, add 35p; over £2, add 75p; over £10, add £1.

☎ (0969) 667566